784

A

AN ANGLER IN ARCADIA

THE FISHERMAN'S TRACK

AN ANGLER IN ARCADIA

BY
WILFRED WALTER MORRIS

THE MORAY PRESS
EDINBURGH & LONDON

FIRST PUBLISHED 1934

THE MORAY PRESS
126 PRINCES STREET, EDINBURGH
39–41 PARKER STREET, KINGSWAY, LONDON

PUBLISHED BY GRANT & MURRAY LIMITED
126 PRINCES STREET, EDINBURGH

PRINTED IN SCOTLAND
BY THE RIVERSIDE PRESS LIMITED, EDINBURGH
BOUND BY
WILLIAM HUNTER & SONS, EDINBURGH

FOREWORD

IT has been said that books about angling resolve themselves into two classes:

Firstly, books full of instruction in the methods of catching fish, methods which, in the writers' views, are infallible. This class of book aims at being intensely practical and matter-of-fact, and is generally profusely illustrated with woodcuts of fishing implements.

Secondly, books which assume that the reader already has some knowledge of the art of fishing with an angle, and are written to give him pleasure when at his ease, maybe by the fireside, or during an idle hour when fishing is not profitable—when fish will not bite, or trout will not rise, or the waters are in winter's grip.

There is, of course, a third class of book, so rare that, when found, it is to be cherished. Of this class is *The Compleat Angler*, in which instruction is given in practical fishing, but in such a manner that the discerning reader is delighted and charmed by the method of instruction, so pleasingly accompanied by naïve comments on men and nature, with literary allusions, and a wealth of quaint out-of-the-common lore.

The first class of angling book to which I have alluded makes little appeal to me. I would liefer study one of the many admirable catalogues issued by fishing-tackle makers of repute. At the cost of a postcard you may get an interesting list of all the latest weapons and apparatus best suited to any branch of the sport, or any kind of water, and you may obtain also plenty of free advice as to where and how to fish.

While I am prepared to admit that the inexperienced fisherman may pick up useful hints from the printed word, to be elaborated and perfected at leisure, I contend he will never learn to fish from a book. Only constant practice with the rod on stream, or loch, or mere, will make the complete fisherman.

In this modest collection of essays connected with fishing—mostly for trout—I have not aimed at being a mentor, nor have I, intentionally, set down anything didactic. I have merely sought to give a few pleasing half-hours to the practised angler who peruses my pages, with the wish that he may enjoy reading of what a brother of the craft, of many years' standing, has observed in his peregrinations by moor, loch and stream; and I also trust that my pages may interest those who, while not claiming to be anglers, are lovers of wild nature. And if, here and there, the novice can cull from these papers a little information which may help him to achieve greater success with the rod—as I hope he may—I shall be all the better gratified.

For the verses I make no apology. It has been the privilege of angling writers to break into rhyme ever since Walton set the example—they may serve to relieve the tension of the narrative element, especially as some of them are not on angling themes. For the imaginative tales there is ample precedent in angling literature.

I have to thank the Editors of *Chambers's Journal*,

FOREWORD

The Fishing Gazette, The Field, The Scottish Field, The Edinburgh Evening News and *The Weekly Scotsman* for permission to reprint some of the essays and verse which have already appeared in their respective publications.

In conclusion, I hope the reader may always have fair fishing weather, with a gentle wind blowing off the bank, and a good water when he goes a-fishing, with " tight lines " to crown his efforts.

CONTENTS

13

CONTENTS

ILLUSTRATIONS

AN ANGLER IN ARCADIA

CHAPTER I

AN ANGLER IN ARCADIA

SOMEWHERE in Arcadia there is a cottage hidden and screened from the fret of the bustling world, with spreading beeches and "immemorial elms" in the background, and beyond them dark Scots firs with red and sturdy stems defying the winter storms and the gales of the equinoctial days.

Before my cottage door is a wide and roomy porch, with settles on each side where I can sit and sort my fishing-tackle, and maybe busk a fly or two for tempting of the speckled trout, and where I can lean my fishing-wand against the wall without troubling to take it to pieces, so that when the opportunity comes, or the urge impels me—an urge which is so seldom resisted—I may take it in hand and saunter down to the singing river, which I can see from my porch, gleaming invitingly not half-a-mile away. For I would not have my river just at my door; there is pleasure in a brief walk with rod a-shoulder and fishing-creel a-back, and I enjoy the few anticipatory moments ere the waterside is reached, full hoping that the trout may be astir.

Around my porch shall be wreathed a wealth of woodbine with its sweet scent in blooming time, and on one side a clematis with its rich purple cups, with bees sipping the nectar from every flower, drowsily humming as they flit from one bloom to another and, full-laden, busily proceed on their way to the hive at the bottom of my garden.

Yes, there is a garden around my cottage, with old-fashioned roses, drenched with fragrance—the moss-rose so seldom seen now, and great blush roses that hang their heads dew-laden in the summer mornings. There are beds of mignonette, and heartsease, and night-scented stock, so that in the cool of the evening, when I sit in my porch at ease, I may glory in the redolent perfume borne on the soft evening air.

There are bushes in my garden, beneath which the jenny-wren builds her downy nest and has no fear of me when I approach now and again to see how she is getting on with the rearing of her tiny and numerous offspring. The pert robin lords it in the hedgerow, and hops through my window betimes in the autumn mornings for a crumb. The thrush and the blackbird and the linnet, and many more of the denizens of the wood behind my cottage, have their bath provided for them near the old sundial, where they playfully splash in a spot where there is no danger from predatory domestic pets, nor do they go hungry when the hard days of winter come, and titbits are ill to find in the fields.

There is joy in a garden which is not too formal, where the flora and fauna blend naturally together, as God intended. What if the blackbirds and thrushes do help themselves to a little fruit in their season? They will sing you a song all the sweeter for it, and in the mornings, while you lie abed awake for a few moments ere rising, you will be rewarded with their music sung in joyous chorus down the aisles of the woodlands.

.   .   .   .

My river, as I have said, is less than half-a-mile
from my porch; and in the quiet nights—and there
is always quiet here save for the hooting of the
owlets or the song of the night-jar, or maybe the
distant yap of a night-hunting fox on the prowl—
you may hear the stream murmuring on its everlasting journey to the sea-gates, tumbling and
splashing against boulders which have been riven
from the rocky hill by frost or flood long, long ago.
My geologist friend says that these boulders were
deposited there by glaciers which melted in our
valley in the Ice Age. He calls them *roches moutonnées*
and, verily, the boulders on the haugh near the
river do appear like sheep in the grey of the morning, or in the gloaming, lazily resting on the green
herbage.

There are halcyon days, too, in the spring, when
nature is beginning to awake, and the sap rises in
the trees; when the early primrose opes its eyes in
the glade, and the sun blinks out between white
fleecy clouds, warming all the earth to life. These
are the days when the river calls me, and in eagerness my rods and reels and my book of hooks and
flies are fondly handled and overhauled, and needful
replenishing is seen to. Then do I hie me to the
river, equipped with all the necessary impedimenta,
ready to seek a few trout in the clear-running limpid
stream.

Since Simon Peter went a-fishing—yea, and
before his time—men have gone down to the waters
to take fish, with net or other means, for augmenta-
tion of the food supply. Our primitive ancestors
used no such refined methods as ours to allure a
few fresh-water fish from the streams or meres.

They had no need, perhaps, as fish must have been in plenty in times so long past, little skill being necessary to secure sufficient unto the day for the family's wants, or for a whole tribe for that matter. Yet with the march of civilization and the necessity of draining the lands for tillage to support an ever-growing population, the physical attributes of the rivers have changed and fish supplies in fresh water have diminished, while the means of catching them have developed into a fine art. And it is only fitting that in the evolutionary process fresh-water fish have become more suspicious of man, their enemy —more educated some will say—and of a verity they seem to become more elusive and difficult to procure, despite the angler's increased skill and cunning as his years of experience grow upon him.

This is all to the good, perhaps, and tends to the preservation of our fish, and a continuation of the means of gentle sport and healthy recreation for those who love to ply a rod on quiet streams. Our ancestors fished for food, as a matter of expediency, but they have handed down to us moderns the instinct of the hunter who seeks a prey. The hunting of fish—of salmon, or sea-trout, or brown trout— has grown into a *cultus* nowadays, especially so where there are trout to be sought, as they seem more intelligent and show more cunning in evading the wiles of the fisherman than do their migratory and perhaps nobler relatives.

Thus do I ruminate as I stroll down to my river this fine May morning. Phyllis, who rules queen over my Arcadian retreat, exhorts me to bring back fish for the table, and I must needs do my utmost to obey her behest, for she is practical, and dearly loves to prepare a dish of comely trout to set before us at breakfast or dinner, deliciously cooked, their pinky-white flesh crisply encrusted with oatmeal.

.　　.　　.　　.　　.　　.　　.

At last I am at the river's side, and to see it purling over the pebbly reaches and swirling round the boulders close at hand delights my eye, and its music is as a sweet song in my ears. The waters are clear, and the sun is warm, and even as I wet my line I perceive a " Blue Dun " fly or two floating down the stream, to be snapped up by rising trout. These are the harbingers of the " rise," a phenom-enon known only to the practical fisherman, to whom it is ever welcome and a pleasing sight. When the conditions are favourable, and the sun's rays shine warmly through the waters, these tiny transient creatures hatch out and rise to the surface, fluttering to rid themselves of their casings, in which they have lain long, and gain freedom for a brief day in the sun-warmed air. 'Tis then that the trout seek them as a dainty food, and it is then that the angler, by imitating the natural insect, endeavours to tempt the unsuspecting trout to their undoing.

Fortune is with me on this occasion—it is not always so—and the reward of my efforts soon begins to evidence itself in the weight of my willow creel. No need for hurry, this vernal day, for in a very short time—or it seems so, although I see by the altered position of the sun, which is now throwing shadows from the woodland trees, that the morning has become afternoon—I have enough trout for our needs. So I desist, since there will be, I hope, other days, and to kill more fish than one needs is surely wanton and unwise. I rest awhile, watching the

river flow on its everlasting way, and with amused
interest observe an old duck, which I had unwittingly disturbed from her nest, making an effort
to lead me away from her treasured eggs by making
pretence of a broken wing and temporary helpless-
ness. It is an old trick of hers, and rather overdone,
and if I were so easy to befool as she thinks, I should
follow her, to find that she is quite strong on the
wing, and as soon as she had induced me far enough
away from her nest she would up and away with
powerful strokes of her pinions.

Later in the month, and when June comes, I
venture seldom on my river when the sun is high
in the heavens, but as evening approaches I take
my wand again and quietly fish until sundown,
picking out a trout here and there with a " Red
Spinner " fly, or an " Olive Dun," from some
ripple or swirl in the shrunken stream. Then as
the dusk comes on I am ready at the big pool for
the evening rise, when trout seem sometimes to
make the still pool boil in their avid attack on the
flies which then appear. This rise is brief as a rule,
and then the trout retire for a calm period in the
shallows until morning dawns.

To the keen fisherman this evening rise is one of
the greatest joys of a summer day's fishing, for oft
the trout will come hungrily to his lures, and he
may take a goodly toll of fish for his creel. The rise
is soon over; but even as the sound of plashing
trout, which has resounded merrily on the still
night air, begins to die gradually away, until it is
no more heard, the dark is coming on, and I
shoulder my rod and retrace my footsteps back to
my cottage.

The exercise and the excitement of my successful fishing have made me healthily weary, and having disposed of my fishing implements in my porch, and hung up my rod, I prepare to sit at my ease and in peace for an hour or two. Phyllis, with gratitude maybe for the addition I have brought to her larder—and how she admired the speckled fish laid out in a row on a large platter for display! —brings me as a reward a stoup of wine, which, verily, in my present healthy weariness, seems to me—

" . . . a beaker full of the warm South,
      Full of the true, the blushful Hippocrene,
      With beaded bubbles winking at the brim "—

and I hold it up to the light so that the rays of the lamp shall shine through and show its delicate hues, then silently and thankfully quaff it, happy in the blessed joy of life in my Arcadian retreat, with those I love who dwell therein.

.   .   .   .

But there are wintry days too in my Arcadia, when the wind soughs through the trees as if moaning for the summer fled, and when the river is a raging torrent roaring along its channel, swollen with the rains from the hill-lands. Then there are days when the frost binds the marge of the river, and the ground is hard frozen; and the cold calm days with a leaden sky from which the snowflakes drop gently, clothing the earth in a pure white mantle, and transforming my garden and the woodlands into fairyland. Was ever scene so fair to look upon as that from my porch on a night when the moon is at full, or on other nights when the stars twinkle brightly on high like gems in a sable setting, and all the world is hushed and at peace?

If I cannot ply my angle wand in these cold and dark days there are other compensations. In my cottage there is a special and cheerful retreat for the winter evenings, where I can browse before a great fire of wooden logs that send out not only warmth but a fragrance born of the woods, the faintly pungent scent of which permeates the air, bringing to mind memories of the charcoal-burning in the forests of other days.

Within my reach are bookshelves adorned with many works of anglers who have long since passed to happier hunting-grounds, and other books by modern writers. Many of these tomes are well-thumbed, and I love to dip into them as the fancy takes me, to live over again with their authors days well spent on river or mere in pursuit of salmon or trout. Father Izaak is there, to con when I may be in a contemplative and meditative mood, and the garrulous old man's ingenuous comments on fish and folk are a delight to read, giving me food for much thinking. I sometimes wonder what success old Izaak would achieve if he could return from the shades to cast a line on our much-fished waters. Walton, however, belonged to a very different age from ours, and it were unwise, maybe, to try to imagine him, with his discursive and leisurely ways, living in these days of rapid movement. There is ever a delight, when one is in the mood, in reading his pleasant discourses, and for these we admire and love him, and are ready to forget or overlook any inaccuracies into which, unwittingly, he may have fallen.

When I would have something of a livelier nature to read, I take down a volume of Charles Kingsley's writings, and peruse his *Chalk Stream Studies*. I am refreshed with Kingsley's breezy optimism and impressed with his erudition. Was there ever such an enthusiastic angler-scholar as was Kingsley? He carries the reader along almost at a gallop; his command of noble English is inspiring; and his apparent enjoyment of life is invigorating to read of. Nothing in nature seemed to escape his keenly observant eye, and he refreshes both the mind and soul, and lays the wonders of life at your feet. 'Tis pity he did not write some real angling songs for us, because such verse as he has written on our sport of angling is but doggerel after all; and he could have written angling songs an he would, for he was dowered with the Muses' divine gift of uttering song.

There was old Tom Stoddart, of Kelso, who had the way of writing angling verse, and in some of his angling songs he thrills with the true spirit and charm of fishing with an angle. A stout-hearted fisherman, who took such catches of salmon and trout as we can never hope to equal in our time, he was skilled and persistent in a superlative degree with his rod, and his writings are still worthy of perusal, even if he was inclined to lay down the law somewhat and tended to be egotistic. If ever an angler lived for his sport, Stoddart did; but we are thankful that he could not fish every day of the year, or he could not have found leisure, from the plying of his rod and line on Tweed and Teviot, to write his angling songs and experiences for the delectation of fishers who have come after him. His daughter has told us that when on one occasion

27

Henry Glassford Bell called to see him, his friend inquired as to what he was doing then. "Doing?" quoth Stoddart, bristling somewhat. "Man, I'm an angler!" And who are ye to blame him, with the Tweed running near his door, and a dozen other streams within easy reach?

Stoddart was one of the giants of an older angling day. Like Kingsley, he was brimming with energy and enthusiasm; but if Kingsley were the greater scholar and more polished writer it seems to me that the Kelso angler-poet was the more practical and successful fisherman.

There are other books it delights me to take down and muse upon for a quiet spell. There are those of "The Amateur Angler," who loved to go a-fishing, and to relate his days of "fishing for pleasure and catching it." He was, perhaps, more of a bookish man than an angler, but his observations on men and fishing and nature are ever worth perusal. And from his quiet books we may turn to "Christopher North," in his sporting jacket, roaring and tearing along; a heroic figure.

Many more books there are in my sanctum in the cottage, and were you with me I could show you some treasures coveted by the bibliophile; but I may not catalogue them here. 'Tis sufficient to tell of the quiet pleasure of conning a book of fishing-lore at slippered ease, to fill the evening of a winter day, and to remind oneself that the dark days will pass and give place to spring again, when the pearly radiance will be on the trees, born of sunshine and April showers, and when trout will be rising in the pools again to the fly.

.   .   .   .

AN ANGLER IN ARCADIA

I hear Phyllis calling me, admonishing me to leave my books for the nonce and join her, which I am ever pleased to do; for she will sing to me some of the old ballads, and maybe tune her violin— since she plays the sweetest of instruments divinely —to some of the sad sweet airs of my country, or rouse me to glee with a Scottish reel or strathspey. For we are in Arcadia, and, when Pan is not piping on his reeds for us in the woodlands, we make merry with our own music in my cottage retreat.

HIS 'PRENTICE HAND

THE OLD MILL LADE

THE OLD MILL LADE

'Tis told 'twas made of old by tonsured friars,
    Who toiled in ancient days (when not at prayer) ;
And from the weir where roar the tumbling waters,
    It still glides gurgling deep, with sleepy purr.

In unripe days its magic banks we haunted
    With baited hook, and wand from neighb'ring tree ;
And, creeping through, where drooping alders flaunted,
    Stealthy, we stalked the fish on crouching knee.

'Tis many a year since then ; but ne'er will fade
    Memories of infant trout caught gleefully ;
Heav'n bless the friars who made the old mill lade,
    Where first we learned how speckled fish to play.

CHAPTER II

HIS 'PRENTICE HAND

THE boy's father was an angler, as was fitting in one who had been born and bred in a land of well-stocked streams and tarns.

Nowadays there were fewer opportunities for fishing. It meant considerable expense going to the distant country for a day's sport, even if the time could be spared. He had other things to think of, now the young son was growing up. So, just to remind himself of still lakes and tarns that mirrored the everlasting hills, and running waters that were ever singing a gay song as they rippled along, he built an aquarium.

The boy watched the construction of the glass case with curious and wondering eyes, and mystery grew upon him as he contemplated the placing of fine gravel and small pebbles in the bottom, and the planting of water-weeds. A cunning little grotto, too, was devised by cementing pieces of pumice-stone together. Then the tank was filled nearly to the top with water.

There came a day when Father brought home a mysterious large can, with perforated lid to let in the air, and he called the boy to come and watch. Together they went to the aquarium with the can, which contained a number of live fishes, and Father transferred them to the glass tank. Some of the fish were golden-hued, and some were silver, and they swam around in a gay and lively way. There were also some bearded loaches, which lay very close to the gravel at the bottom of the tank, and you could scarcely tell they were there.

The boy could not keep away from this new wonder, and would gaze into it for long spells, delighting to see the fishes dart about when he tapped on the glass. Sometimes they would hide in the grotto, and at times he was allowed to feed them with bread crumbs, or grubs, or ants' eggs, until they became quite tame.

Later on, Father brought home one or two newts, or efts, and put them on top of the grotto, which stood just out of the water. But the boy was not very sure that he liked newts. They were too much like young crocodiles or alligators, about which he had heard fearsome stories of ferocity. No, he did not like the newts at all.

Then Father put some tiny insects on the water —shiny water-beetles with lovely green wings, and some insects that scooted about jerkily, which he called " boatmen." And there were water-snails that crawled up the inside of the glass, and a few fresh-water shrimps and other small things. The boy couldn't remember all their names, but they were very interesting. One day one of the goldfish jumped clean out of the water, on to the floor. The cat got away with it, and there was grief.

And so began the boy's first acquaintance with fish and some aquatic creatures.

. . . . . .

At a short distance from the village school there was a large reservoir, originated by the simple

expedient of building a great stone dam or embank-
ment at the lower end of a depression between two
hills. It was fed by the water from a small stream
and several natural springs which bubbled from
the hillsides.

The shallow end of the reservoir was a great
and happy hunting-ground to which the small boys
resorted after school hours in summer-time. The
water there was alive with little fish—sticklebacks
(the " tiddler " of the London urchin) and minnows
and loaches being predominant. Great was the
pride of a young sportsman if he caught a fine fat
stickleback with a gay red throat—such were called
" doctors "—to put into the glass jar to carry home;
and if a loach or two added variety to the catch
he was the envy of his fellows, as loaches were so
elusively slippery, and wriggled out of the little
hands so easily. They had neither rod nor line to
fish with; they just groped after the poor harassed
fish with their hands, chasing them into little
shallow bays from whence there was scant chance
of their escaping.

Other phases of life there were down near the
reservoir that drew the young folk thence in spring
and summer. There was a patch of marshy ground
with a small pond, where bulrushes sent up their
tall spikes, and yellow irises grew in profusion, and
where frogs congregated in hundreds to lay their
spawn, to be succeeded later by the quaint tadpoles,
which seemed nearly all head. It was of course quite
the accustomed thing to carry home a big jar full
of these queer creatures. These were usually kept
in the garden, and their development into wee frogs
watched for daily. But it was very strange and

puzzling—they seemed to disappear one by one until none were left. The boys believed that the tadpoles ate each other up!

The marshy land near the water was a great place to see the wonderful dragon-fly, with its big head and great eyes and long thin body. What beautiful gauzy wings it had, and how it glistened in the sunshine! One of these wonders of creation was a trophy greatly coveted but seldom acquired. Big bumble-bees, some reeling drunk with the nectar sipped from the thistle blooms and wild flowers on the marsh, were easier prey, and the poor foolish creatures were trapped and imprisoned in wooden matchboxes just for the fun of hearing their buzzing. They were generally liberated before much harm befell them, as the buzzing became rather monotonous and tiresome.

The boy was getting on, and his young mind was already unconsciously absorbing knowledge, of an elementary kind, relating to the wild life around him, little dreaming of the fascination it would have for him in future years.

The time came when the boy discovered an old hollow-cane fishing-rod in the lumber-room, and some fishing hooks and lines: a veritable case of treasure trove, notwithstanding that the hooks were rather rusted. He had got beyond the stickleback stage now, and began to dream of catching bigger fish.

There were several ponds and old quarry-holes within an easy walk from his home, some of them reputed to contain great big fish. At least, the older boys said so; and, in due course, short excursions were arranged, and many hours were spent watching quill floats; but they never caught anything, so concluded they had been misled.

However, there was a little river not very far away, fairly free from pollution, and clear. Rumour said that it had been a good trout stream at one time. There was no reason to doubt rumour in this instance, but it must have been many many years since trout were there in anything like numbers sufficient to fill a creel. Still, the boy's mind was not concerned with the ancient piscatory history of the stream, and he meant to try his fortune. So he took his rod and some bait—maggots and small worms— and fished the swims carefully, as he had seen men doing on several occasions.

Nothing happened for a long time. Then, when he was beginning to weary a bit, he had the glorious sensation of seeing his float agitated violently, and then go under water. He was of course fishing without a reel, and he jerked the poor fish out of the water on to the bank. He did not know that he had got quite a notably rare specimen for that river—it was a Miller's Thumb, sometimes known as a " Tommy Logge." He had never seen such a queer-looking fish before, with its huge head so much out of proportion to its body. He thought it a horrid-looking beast, and with extreme disgust shook it off the hook back into the water.

.   .   .   .

There came a time, during a holiday away from home, when opportunity arose for gaining more experience, and some very innocent perch were captured in a hill tarn by our young angler, with his primitive tackle. It was exciting fun pulling out the bright-coloured perch one after another, and it was a proud young fisherman who arrived home with quite a nice catch which could be cooked and put on the breakfast-table.

The most exciting event about this period occurred one day when he took his old rod and tackle to try his fate in a mill lade. He knew there were trout in the river from whence the lade's water came, but he did not think he could reach them with his short line, and an old rod that would not throw a long line accurately if he had one. He had been observing local fly-fishers on the river, too, and wished he had a fly-rod.

However, like a wise philosopher, he made the best of what he had, and cast his line in the gurgling depths of the old mill stream.

He had no sooner dropped a worm-baited hook into the water than a great trout—great to him, although it was under a pound weight—grabbed it, and was immediately hooked. It was all so sudden that he got quite a fright, as the trout made a great to-do and splashed angrily about for some moments.

The youngster held tight, wondering in his mind what to do, as the trout was too heavy to lift right out and up a steep bank. The fish, however, decided for him, as it gave a great wallop with its tail, and broke away, taking a few yards of line and the quill float. It made a rush up the mill lade and managed to get into the mill pond, where the boy, with mixed feelings, watched it for quite a while swimming about with the line and gaily-coloured float dragging behind betraying its whereabouts.

After this sad experience there was nothing for it but to acquire a real serviceable trout-rod, with

a proper reel and line, and some flies. He felt
confident that he could soon learn to cast a fly
accurately, and play a fish in the correct way, as he
had seen a fisherman doing often on an artificial trout
lake near home.

So it came about that his father bought him a
greenheart rod, and the rest of a fly-fisher's outfit,
and gave him some hints on how to tie his flies on,
and how and where to cast them without making a
splash on the surface of the water.

Every angler can look back with pleasure to one
glorious day in his early fishing career, a day that
stands out above all others—the day when he first
triumphed over a wonderful sporting fish, whether
salmon, trout, or one of the so-called (but, to my
mind, unfairly so) " coarse " fish.

Now it happened that our young angler went
forth to the river one day, full of courage and the
hope of landing some of the trout he had seen rising
at the flies on the water. At the back of his mind
was a vague sort of feeling that he would like to
catch a real big one, and then he could show his
friends that he was a right and proper fisherman
who knew the game, and not one of those fellows
who pottered about the water and never caught
anything worth creeling.

To digress, I may mention that there were sea-
trout in the river. This the boy did not know, as he
had yet to learn nearly all there was to know about
migratory fish. His father, fortunately for the boy,
had remembered this when he gave him his fishing
outfit, and the line and cast were purposely chosen
for their strength, and would hold a good-sized fish.

The youngster was fishing gently down the river,

throwing his cast across the water and allowing his flies to float downstream, as he had seen the local fishermen doing. He had fished for an hour or two with exemplary patience, and had not caught anything worth taking away, when, at the tail of a deep pool, he felt, rather than saw, there was something at the end of his line.

Impulsively he raised his rod-point with somewhat of a jerk. With an experienced fisherman such carelessness would probably have resulted in the hook leaving the mouth of the fish, but the boy had unconsciously struck from the reel, and the hook luckily held.

Then the fun began. The reel screeched, and the fish went off with a merry spin down the river, the line running off the reel at great speed. The boy followed as quickly as he could, and then the fish stopped its wild career, and flung itself into the air —a glittering silvery gleam. The line was slack now, and the boy dreaded lest he had lost his fish, but on reeling up his line found that it was still on.

As soon as the fish felt the pull of the tightened line, off it went again, upstream this time, until it was well above where the boy stood. But he held it, and then began a series of wild jumps and flurries, after which the fish bored to the bottom.

The problem of how he was to land such a big wild fish began to worry the boy, as he had no net.

Yet he was not without resource. About thirty or forty yards below him was a nice bank of gravel, with a gentle slope into the river, and he had seen others play their fish and then guide them through a shallow on to this gravel, gently dragging them into safety. So he determined this was his best plan, and, holding his rod well up, he induced or led the fish, now becoming spent, towards the gravel slope. After a final dash to get away, the fish began to turn on its side, and the boy triumphantly dragged it gently ashore.

It was a fine sea-trout. When the boy reached home it was weighed, and found to turn the scale at three and a half pounds.

He was a proud youth as he showed his capture to his pleased father. He had won his spurs—if one may borrow a metaphor from another sport—and never has he forgotten the ecstasy and exhilaration of that first sea-trout.

Another lifelong angler was made that day, and the 'prentice hand had claimed his place as a skilled craftsman.

A FINE WEEK—AND A
WET DAY

ENCOURAGEMENT

A good trout rises to the flies
Just o'er yon eddy blown—
Maybe we'll take him by surprise,
With " Greenwell " fly well thrown !

He has it ! and well-hooked, I swear !
He rushes for yon weed !
Now hold him firm, and have a care,
Or he will soon be freed.

He leaps and turns and tries to break
The slender tapering line;
Then round a rock, with angry shake,
The trace he would entwine.

He's tiring out; be gentle now,
Then lead him down the stream;
Now deftly place the net below,
The silv'ry flashing gleam.

A gallant " pounder," safely creeled,
Starts well our angling day—
We'll try that pool again: 't may yield
A bigger trout to play !

THE TWEED ABOVE MELROSE

[*page* 48

CHAPTER III

A FINE WEEK—AND A WET DAY

WE often met, the two of us, for a fortnight's trout-fishing together in the early spring, and we generally had the good fortune to find fair sport somewhere.

A fortnight, indeed, was all too short; but a lot of fishing can be crammed into two weeks if the angler be enthusiastic and active, and finds the right water.

Amidst the city's fretful, never-ceasing noise and bustle, the anticipation of a spring holiday always makes the daily round and common task seem easier, and lifts one up towards visions of sylvan scenes through which run crystal streams where speckled trout abound and never fail to rise; and one dreams of beloved haunts soon to be visited again with a rod, of feeling the bracing air of the north on the cheeks, and of filling smoke-dried lungs with refreshing, keen pure air.

Well, we had forgathered once again, with plans made for our fishing the most interesting river I know—interesting historically as well as piscatorially. With great good luck we had obtained leave to fish several delightful and more or less preserved stretches of the river, giving us a variety of scene and sport.

It may be selfish of me—anglers, I fear, sometimes

are inclined to be so—and, although it is many years ago, it is not my intention here to reveal where our fishing took place, except that the waters were famous ones, and across the Scottish Border.

I still see, in my mind's eye, that peerless stretch of the river, the shelving strand fringing the edge of a pool which gradually deepened towards the opposite bank, whereunder the big trout lay taking toll of the insects which floated down or dropped from the overhanging trees and bushes; the high scaur behind, verdantly clad with scrubby woods and fernery, where the hawk had its eyrie, and below leading to a wide glade carpeted with countless wild hyacinths diffusing an intoxicating scent around, and rippling blue like the sea under a summer sky of azure. Then the tail of the pool branched off into a succession of broken streams, beating against rocky boulders, behind which deep eddies formed where trout could always be found. After the streams the river converged into a narrow gorge, making a mighty sweep round a bend, then placidly broadening out between leafy woods and flowery meads. Surely there was no fairer spot to gladden the eye of a fisherman or lover of rural beauty.

It was past mid-April. March had been wild and blustering, with plenty of rain, so that the river-beds were well scoured and clean, and there was an ample flow of water. April was typical of the month, so far as alternate rain and sunshine could make it so. The mornings would begin with bright skies, clouding over after a while, bringing showers of cold rain, and even at times hail or sleet, only to clear up again and to leave all nature smiling as if through tears.

The knowing angler is best pleased with an April day that begins well with intermittent sunshine, for it generally prognosticates an early hatch of flies, and that trout will commence to rise about ten of the clock or so, perhaps to continue, on and off, more or less spasmodically, until four in the afternoon.

If, however, the sun shines too brightly and powerfully for the whole morning it is an ill omen, for the March Browns have then a disconcerting way of hatching out in such swarms that the river seems to become covered with speckled brown, and for a very brief spell the pools are a-boil with rising trout. In such conditions the fisherman has but a poor chance of hooking fish with his artificial fly, whether he presents it to them " wet " or " dry," for his imitation is scarcely noticed by the trout when there are thousands of the real insect floating by.

Perhaps that is the reason, or maybe trout are shrewd enough to discriminate between the imitation and the genuine fly when there are so many indubitably natural ones with which to compare the fake. However that may be, it is tantalizing enough to throw a fly at rising trout and never feel a " rug," when the pool is alive with feeding fish, rising around you. Generally speaking, the angler may just as well reel up his line for a while when the March Browns swarm in their myriads, then light his pipe, and contemplate nature.

Sometimes, when the phenomenon of the March Brown swarm is taking place, I have found some little success by changing my fly, and I have known the trout to take a Brown Partridge Hackle fly, or

" Spider," well sunk, even when the fish were rising madly to the March Browns on the surface. A Blue Dun spider, too, I have on one or two occasions found useful in similar circumstances—resorted to, I must confess, more as an experiment or desperate measure, rather than because I had reasoned out that such a fly might allure the trout.

Yet one never knows, in trout-fishing, what vagaries the trout will perform. I remember once creeling a nice lot of trout on a Greenwell's Glory that was minus wings and was so much worn with usage that there was practically little left but the hook and body. But that is a story for another time.

'Twould be tedium to read, no less than to write, of each day we fished : one day, generally speaking, is so much like another to read of, although actually each day brings its own experiences and incidents, which seem ever new at the time.

I will therefore describe one of our days, as being typical of the rest of them that we spent together.

So let us get on with the fishing. We have three or four good miles to walk before we reach our water, so we are up early on our first day, eager to wet our lines, and full of hope.

It is the last week of April, and a fine morning— not too bright and with a few grey clouds scudding well above the hill-tops. This is pleasing, for we have a tradition that if the hill-tops are capped with cloud we shall catch few fish.

At last we reach the waterside, and find the river clear and in good trim, and with a good volume of water, as we had hoped. In two or three weeks

from now, in the absence of much rain, it will
have shrunk to summer-level, and trout will be
hard to come by, with the fly, in the daytime.

What flies shall we try? That is the first question
which crops up. We shall fish the wet fly to-day,
the water being fairly heavy, and as trout will be seen
rising only for a brief period of the day. Usually
at this time of the year trout will take a fly at any
time between 10 A.M. and 4 P.M., but much depends
on the amount of sunshine we get. If the sun be
bright in the early part of the day, there so often
happens the big hatch of fly about noon, a great
boil of trout in every pool, and then the rise is very
quickly over, and not another dimple may be seen
on pool, or splash of tail in streamy water.

So we put up a cast of three flies, with a March
Brown as tail fly. My companion suggests a Blue
Dun for second fly, and a Grey Spider, with yellow
body, as dropper. While I agree with the March
Brown as leading fly, I decide on a Greenwell's
Glory for second fly and a Partridge Hackle, with
claret body, for my dropper.

A few words about the March Brown will not
be out of place here. It is a good standby as a fly
almost at any time of the season, but especially in
April. But have a care, when you are dressing it
—if so be that you dress your own flies—or when
obtaining it from your favourite fly-dresser, that it
is not too large and feathery.

A March Brown on a No. 1 hook is quite large
enough for trout, and it should not have too much
hackle. For the March Brown, after all, is but one
of the smaller ephemeridæ, delicate in outline and
graceful of limb, and to represent it by a bunch of

hackle like a broom is to insult the trout by under-estimating their discriminating powers.

An old fisherman who used to supply me with flies protested when I insisted that his March Browns on No. 3 and No. 4 hooks were too big. He said he had known the pattern as he dressed it for over fifty years. I pointed out that I never had sport worth mentioning with these big flies, and would prefer them on No. 1 hooks. The female March Brown is generally more attractive to the trout than the male, and an olive-bodied, ginger-hackled March Brown will be found useful at all times, if dressed on the small hooks, and with a sparing hand when putting on the hackle. At any rate, that has been my experience.

And so fall to our sport. There is nothing moving yet, not a sign of a rise anywhere; but that does not daunt the wet-fly fisherman who knows where the trout are lying.

My companion has gone away up-river to fish some fine deep-running streams, on the edges of which good trout are to be got, and, if you can reach across the streams with a longish line, or by wading, you are sure to get trout of goodly proportions if they are to be tempted at all.

Where I commence there is a long, broad pool, deepening to the far side, and with a gently sloping bank of gravel, easy to wade, with a gravel strand behind me up which it is safe to drag a trout gently after playing him.

There are some big trout in this pool, and, albeit I have not yet perceived any indication of anything moving, I soon hook a fish at the head of the pool. It gives me a good run before it is drawn up the gravel, and weighs well over half-a-pound, being in excellent condition. It was hooked on the Greenwell.

When we came down to the water there was a blustering wind blowing, a wind such as we often get in the north at the tail-end of April; but now it has dropped, the sun is shining, and there is warmth and mellowness in the air. As if the sunshine had drawn them out of some hiding-place, the flies are now beginning to show on the water, and *plop! plop!* one can hear as the trout rise over to the far side of the pool, below the overhanging branches of a larch-tree.

A long line, thrown true, and a fly dropped gently, a foot or two above a feeder, deceives him, and he soon joins his fellow in the creel; a " pounder " this time, and a worthy tribute to the March Brown.

Now the trout are having a merry carnival. The pool seems alive with them, eager to assimilate the March Browns which are thickly covering the water. The stream carries them over to the other bank, and I wade in as far as my waders will permit, casting a long line almost to the other side.

There are too many of the real flies about for the fish to take much notice of my artificial flies, but nevertheless I get a trout now and again—trout of half-a-pound, and three-quarters, and one or two nearer a pound, until I have about a dozen of excellent fish—not a great basket, perhaps, but a creel of seven pounds or thereby to begin the season with is not to be despised, and I am duly elated.

The Greenwell's Glory, strangely enough, has

accounted for most of them, and the Partridge Hackle has taken its share. The March Brown, as so often happens when there is an abundance of the natural fly, did very little execution.

The rise was of very short duration, and although for a quarter of an hour or so the sport was lively and exciting, as soon as the big hatch of flies had passed the trout were quiet again, and not a dimple disturbed the still surface of my pool.

I fished on for a little while without any responsive " rug," and then reeled up my line. Then I went upstream, to see how my companion was faring. His experience had been not unlike my own, although the average weight of his ten fish was a little higher than mine.

We had a short rest while we took a frugal lunch. It was after one o'clock—time had passed quicker than we thought—and still there were no trout moving; but we decided to fish on until about four o'clock. Then we separated again, my friend going down the water, while I went up above.

By now the weather was becoming decidedly cooler. Clouds were gathering, and the wind rising. I thought, however, that I might be able to get one or two fish in the tails of pools which I knew of, especially if there was a ripple caused by the breeze.

I fished every likely spot, but the colder air seemed to have put the trout down and off the fly. I did, however, succeed in landing two or three nice little trout good enough for the creel, besides having a run with a biggish fish which, from the way it leaped out of the water, I took to be a sea-trout. To my regret it broke my light tackle and got away.

Then down came the rain, and a wild blatter of hailstones, chilling the air and making conditions very unpleasant for a time; yet it was soon over and the sun shone out again, making the buds on the trees, as yet barely sprouting, gleam like Orient pearls as the light caught the raindrops on them.

We desisted, as arranged, about four o'clock. We might have fished on—I have sometimes done well on a day like this at a later hour—but we were satisfied for the first day, for had we not nearly a fortnight yet to come?

Comparing our catches, I had just fourteen trout, weighing seven pounds and three-quarters in all, and the other rod's " take " was a very similar one.

And so the days went on, a nice basket each, on each day we went out; and, without making very strenuous efforts for big catches, our combined catch each day came generally to about fifteen pounds.

Then came Friday. We woke up to find a dull morning, with rain beginning to fall quietly, steadily, persistently. There was no perceptible wind. It was mild, and I thought that if the rain did not soon cease the river would rise, and there would be an end to all hopes of catching trout with a fly. It scarcely seemed to me worth while getting a thorough wetting, with little chance of sport, and as I had a letter or two to write, and some fishing-tackle to see to—casts to make up, and a rod-top to repair—I decided not to make the journey.

My friend, with ironic remarks about a fisherman who funked a wetting, announced his intention of trying his luck, and away he went, with my best wishes for tight lines; but, truth to tell, never in my secret mind did I think he would meet with them.

The rain kept on, and I had visions of my poor friend on a river discoloured and in spate, and I shook hands with myself for my superior weather-wisdom, and for staying at home out of the misery of it all.

I stood at the front door at about five o'clock watching that quiet steady downpour, and thinking about the poor fellow at the waterside. Then I saw a weary-looking, bedraggled and thoroughly wet creature come with back bowed through the garden gate. He seemed as if he could scarce drag one foot after the other.

Not a word did he utter as he passed on his way to the back regions, where we usually deposited our gear, but beckoned me to come along. I seized his creel and, feeling its weight, I had a surprise. It was a creel capable of holding twenty-five pounds of trout, and it was crammed full!

We got two great platters from the kitchen, and piled the trout on them—a noble lot of fish such as I had seldom seen from an April day's fishing; big plump trout, most of them, and the total weight was just under twenty-five pounds.

He told me later in the evening that he could have caught as many fish as he wished, and more than he could have carried. A Blue Dun spider and a Partridge Hackle fly had taken most of them, and the fish had taken the flies at almost every cast from the hour he commenced, as if they meant to get all the flies they could before the flood came.

The curious thing was that the water did not

rise, as it would have done had the rains been heavy in the uplands, and it seemed as if the rainfall was only local.

I have fished through pouring rain many times, and I have wended my way home with the water literally running into my boots, but I never had the luck to strike a day like that. Which shows —what every angler knows—how often it is the unexpected that happens when trout-fishing.

A DISH OF TROUT

THE HILL BURN

Child of the grey mist
And the cool night-dew;
Born 'midst the heather,
Where wails the curlew;
Dripping from riven crag
Down the lone mountain,
Limpid thy waters—
Nature's pure fountain.

Fed by the moss hag's
Amber-gold offspring;
Seeking the low land,
Ever strength gathering;
Heedless, thy waters—
Hurriedly leaving
Haunts of thy youth's days—
A wayward course weaving.

Oft have I wooed thee
With angle and creel,
Glad when my angling
Brought song from my reel;
But thou sing'st for ever,
Pursuing thy quest
For life's great river,
O child of the mist!

CHAPTER IV

A DISH OF TROUT

IN the late 1890's, as did "Wullie Wastle" of the old song, I dwelt on Tweed; and, besides having access to many of the best reaches of that noble angling river, I oft ventured farther afield to ply my rod on other waters.

To be precise, it was in the year 1898 that I had been fishing the Cowdenknowes section of the River Leader, on a fine day in May, and I had been successful in creeling a nice basket of that stream's lovely trout, which, when in condition, have almost the bright-hued colouring of the perch, and the flesh of them is as pink as that of salmon-trout.

Shortly before this time I had been corresponding with the late Mr William Senior, better known perhaps to anglers as "Red Spinner," who was then the angling editor of *The Field*, and later on editor-in-chief of that well-known paper.

So it came to pass that, having trout at my disposal, I sent enough for a "fry"—as the Borderer would say—to "Red Spinner." I had not known that he had been ill, but he wrote me a charming letter of thanks for the fish, saying that he had had a wearying illness, and was just recovering, with a tonic-made appetite; while he emphasized how welcome and valuable an unexpected treat of this kind was to him. He mentioned that they recalled to his memory a basket of somewhat similar fish he had taken the last time he had fished the Teviot.

I am reminded of all this by the action of a kind and considerate friend who, the other day, sent me " a dish of trout " from the Tweed. They had been caught one July night and dispatched to me in London with all speed, arriving quite fresh, and in time for luncheon. I had been mewed up in bed for many months, somewhat helpless, and I must confess rather jaded with the ordinary dietary of an invalid. The trout were therefore a pleasant change in the way of food, served up cooked in the Scottish way, well sprinkled with oatmeal, hot and crisply browned.

When I opened the parcel on its arrival a strange nostalgia overcame my senses, and the smell which arose from the trout and the " wild rhubarb " leaves in which they had been wrapped to keep them fresh—not always a wise thing, this wrapping in greenstuff—seemed like a breath direct from the riverside. I had only to close my eyes to imagine I was on the banks of the Tweed in the dusk of a late summer evening, with the fresh-water aroma arising from the water's edge as I waded quietly along the rim of a pool, crushing the water-weeds with my brogues, and breaking a few stems in the forest of reeds by the stream's brink as I pushed them aside, peering out on the still pool to see if any fish were rising at the evening flies.

In my mind's eye arose a vision of a jungle of wild rhubarb almost oxter-high, and dockens, and the muddy pool at the foot of the brae a few yards from the river, where the frogs croaked their melancholy song in early spring when they were about their business of laying spawn; and I had a fleeting memory of the close of a warm summer day when the heavy smell of vegetation decaying by the fringe of the stream, and in the darker places of the woods, was carried up by the dank steamy mist beginning to arise after the sun had set.

There is no mistaking this fresh-water smell. Sometimes, when passing along a busy thoroughfare in the town, when one's thoughts have been of anything but of fishing, or riverside life, a faint scent will catch the sensory nerves of smell, and at once comes to the mental vision of the angler-pedestrian a scene of rippling waters and rising trout, and then suddenly one is aware of passing a fishmonger's shop, with his finny wares exposed to the air, and on the slab is a small heap of fresh trout grouped round a lump of ice.

I have heard it said of travellers who have been much in Eastern lands that, when passing some great emporium in the City, or maybe getting to windward of a ship unloading merchandise at a riverside wharf, they may catch a whiff of some Eastern smell, and their minds at once cast back to the Orient, while they momentarily imagine they are in the East again, with its spicy garlic smells, and they hear the East a-calling them.

The angler is in like case—a whiff of something comes to his nostrils, and at once he is transported on a magic carpet to some beloved riverside, hundreds of miles away, perhaps; and he lives over again, in memory, some incident which happened to him when fishing years ago, maybe half-a-lifetime away.

.   .   .   .

67

Whenever I see or smell garlic I am reminded of one fine day in early spring when I went a-fishing at Old Melrose. I had fished the flats, as I went up the river, without a great deal of success. The day was yet young, and there had been no show of fly to induce the trout to move, and consequently no "rise." So I left the river's brim to make a detour through the wood, intending to try some roughish water higher up. The winding path made a steep ascent, and from the high ground I could see the water down below quite clearly.

I had not gone very far when I observed what was a palpable rise of a good fish, so I looked for a favourable spot from whence I could descend the rocky bank safely, and get down to the water again. Just below the path was a scree, formed by the denudation of the rocky bank, sloping at a very sharp angle, but not too steep, it seemed, to prevent my essaying the descent. Down below were great rocks, and a pleasant-looking patch of greenery, and starry white flowers showing up with prominence, not without a distinctive beauty, for, after all, the bloom of the garlic is a pretty one.

Well, I stepped down from the path to the top of the scree, but no sooner was my weight upon it than I began a glissade, with the scree tumbling down behind me in an avalanche of rocks and stones. Of course, I was fully equipped with all the usual impedimenta of a fisherman—waders, heavy brogues, creel, landing-net and fishing-rod —so that I was more or less helpless, and had to go with the avalanche.

I reached the bottom in very quick time, and rolled over for several yards through a bed of wild garlic which grew there in great profusion; and as I crushed the brittle and juicy stems in my progress a very pungent smell rose all around me, and my clothing gathered up and absorbed the strong-smelling and pervading sap from the bruised plants.

Eventually I picked myself up and assembled my belongings, and ere long I was plying my rod assiduously on the glorious, rock-strewn pools, where some fine trout were rising. I cannot say whether the overpowering stink of garlic was transmitted through the water in any way to attract the trout; but I do know that I had a very fine basket of trout to take home, most of them about three-quarters of a pound in weight—a most excellent average.

.   .   .   .

Whenever the smell of peppermint floats to me on the air—as it has not seldom done in the kirk on a Scottish sabbath, say from some douce body, an elder most likely, listening intently to the sermon, and surreptitiously sucking a peppermint sweetie, or from some sonsy farm lass who is whiling away the tedium of the minister's discourse in the same fashion, or even from the aroma from the prosaic mint sauce served up as a relish to the succulent lamb partaken of at dinner—I have mental visions of days with my fishing-rod at Gledswood in the months of May and June.

Some little distance below the confluence of the Leader Water and the Tweed there used to grow, in luxuriance, a great bank of spearmint, and I recollect being there with a friend just before the war. He was preceding me down the river, and as he went along he walked through the bed of spearmint, from which the invigorating smell arose and floated up to me as I followed him. I culled a few sprigs and placed them in my creel to freshen it up.

On that occasion too we had some excellent sport with the trout, and now when I smell pepper-mint I think of Gledswood, and one of the bonniest bits of the Tweed; and Gledswood is always associated in my mind with an adventure I had in which a noble trout of two and a half pounds was concerned.

In *The Book of the Dry Fly*, the author, in dis-cussing " the not unequal contest " between the angler and the trout, says it is a curious thing that, however seemingly dead-beat, a trout which has been played and becomes detached from the hook, when just on the point of being netted, always has enough energy left to avail himself of this mishap, and to depart before the net has enclosed his shining sides. Mr Dewar confesses that, although he has always " stretched lame hands " on such an occasion, he has never come near to recovering a once-released trout, and goes on to say there are very few people who have ever been successful in landing a trout after the hold of the hook has given way.

But my whiff of spearmint reminds me that I have on at least one memorable occasion been more fortunate than the author of *The Book of the Dry Fly*.

I had been fishing at Gledswood for some hours one day near the end of April. While I had not been very successful, yet I had a few nice trout in my creel. A few hundred yards lower down the river than my bed of spearmint I hooked a good trout which raced away down the river, in a fairly strong stream. The hook seemed to be well in, and I felt confident I should land my fish safely; but the trout took me down to where I could not wade further. I was then in the middle of the river, in a pool which lapped the banks, and there was no friendly strand of shelving gravel near by. Between me and the bank the water was shallow, and behind me were high fir-trees, with low-hanging branches dipping almost to the tree-roots, from which the soil had been washed away by flood-waters.

The trout was apparently played out, and I backed towards the bank, intending to net my quarry in the shallow water. As I held my rod up, to keep a reasonable pressure on the line, the top piece caught on a branch of the fir behind me, and my line became entangled on the tree.

I was in a quandary, as I had no control over the trout whatsoever, and he seemed to know it as well as I did. He was just beyond the reach of my landing-net, which I had been holding in readiness as I reeled in the line. Another foot or so and I could have netted him. He began to flurry and splash, and his powerful tail struck the line: the hook came away, and the trout was free.

For a moment I lost hope. The trout was fully visible, and, feeling himself free of the barb, he turned round ever so deliberately, and then, with a strong flick of his tail, he made a desperate dash for the deep water.

I have said I had my net in readiness, so, with one mighty sweep, with outstretched arm, letting the butt of my rod fall into the river, I dashed after the trout, bringing the mouth of my net, as it happened, directly in front of him. He ran straight into it, and in a twinkling I was wading out of the river with my capture.

The trout weighed two and a half pounds, and he really deserved to get away. Indeed, I had qualms afterwards as to whether I had been guilty of an unsportsmanlike act in netting him; but there is not time to think of the ethics of the game on an occasion of this kind, and the instincts of the hunter to secure his prey, which seem to be dormant in most of us, come out on top.

.   .   .   .

On the first occasion on which I fished a well-known and picturesque section of the Leader Water, whereon I have frequently since then had great sport with trout—and, I must own, from which I have sometimes returned with an empty creel—I received a shock to my olfactory nerves, and also my æsthetic senses.

It was a warm summer day. Down by the water-side there was ample shade given by the foliage of towering trees on one side, and, as the water ran at the foot of deep scaurs on the opposite side, there was always shelter from the sun's rays at the river-level a few hours after noontide.

As I cast my fly over a rising fish, intent on my sport, I was suddenly aware of an offensive effluvium, and, looking around for the cause, soon discovered from whence it came. Almost opposite to where I stood, and high up the scaur, almost screened by vegetation, was the orifice of a sewer, and it was pouring its unspeakably foul contents down the face of the scaur into the pool I was fishing. I ascertained that this was the sewer from the mansion-house and stables on the estate, and, as there was no attempt whatsoever to treat the sewage in any way, the crude effluent was polluting the sylvan Leader, and also causing a distinct blemish in a lovely piece of scenery. 'Tis true, 'tis pity; but pity 'tis, 'tis true, that such things should be, as it would be such a simple matter for every country house to treat its own sewage, at little or no expense except a small initial outlay, so that the effluent from the sewer would be innocuous, and inoffensive to sight or smell, and would not pollute a sparkling stream.

I have recollections of fishing in the Teviot many miles below Hawick, when the river was low in summer-time. The river-bed was covered with a layer of grey, flocculent matter, which, at every step taken when I waded, rose in an offensive cloud, rendering the water milky in hue, and giving off a most disagreeable smell. Indeed it was so offensive that I had to give up fishing. There seemed to be few trout about, and I was not surprised, for the natural food of trout could not survive the poisons floating down from the mills of Hawick.

It is fortunate that fresh running water has the power of purifying itself as it tumbles about in rocky streams and meanders along weed-strewn flats, given that the pollution is not too heavy and frequent; but there is no reason why streams, such as the Border country is abundantly provided with, should ever become the multicoloured abominations smelling to heaven that one sees in the thickly-

populated industrial areas of Lancashire and
Yorkshire.

> " Deil tak the dirty trading loon
>   Wad gar his water ca' his wheel,
>   And drift his dyes and poisons doon
>   By fair Tweedside, at Ashiestiel ! "

.   .   .   .

The angler on the Scottish side of the Border will
seldom meet with the sweet-scented violet in his
rambles through the woodlands or by the stream-
side; but often here in town, when I pass the laden
flower-sellers in the early spring, I catch the fragrance of the violets they sell, and there come across
my memory thoughts of a day, many years ago,
when I fished at Old Melrose and Bemersyde in
early summer.

It was a warm day, and the air was humid, the
scent of wild flowers—meadow-sweet, sweetbrier
and hawthorn—hung heavily in the air. But, as I
gradually worked my way up the water, I left these
scents behind me, and I was soon passing over
rocky, barren ground, where nothing but mosses
and lichens seemed to grow, with perhaps here
and there a few king-cups shining with their golden
blooms on a gravel-bed from which the water had
receded owing to the early summer drought, or the
gay willow herb showed its bright spikes of bloom
springing from stony ground.

A delicious perfume suddenly assailed my nostrils.
Surely, I thought, this is the smell of sweet violets;
but I had never known of the real sweet-scented
variety growing in this locality. Plenty of the
scentless, dog-tooth violets could be found in
primrose time, peeping shyly from amongst the

primroses on the sunny brae, beneath blackthorn and sweetbrier, but never the delicious perfumed violet of more southern climes.

So I began to search, and, oh, joy! there was a great and glorious bed of very pale blue violets, almost white, and I flung myself ruthlessly down amongst them, absorbing their heavenly fragrance, admiring their delicate and modest beauty until I was intoxicated with delight. Over the water, in a tree on the other bank of the river, a thrush was pouring out his mellifluous song from a full and happy heart, and in a bramble-bush near me a green linnet hopped about twittering uneasily, as if wondering what I was doing.

At last I had to tear myself away—for had I not really come here to fish for trout?—in spite of my sentimental love of the dainty and exquisite blooms, for

> " To me the meanest flower that blows can give
> Thoughts that do often lie too deep for tears."

I fear, after all, that my violets were not indigenous to the country: not native Borderers. They had probably sprung from some alien plant thrown out with garden rubbish, dumped on the riverside, to be washed away in the next convenient flood, only to be deposited lower down, where the plant took root and spread and flourished in the rich alluvium by the waterside.

I have not visited that sweet spot for many years; but I often wonder if my bed of pale, sweet-scented violets still flourishes, to enchant some passing and, maybe, sentimental angler who is out to obtain " a dish of trout."

HANDICAPPED ANGLERS

IGNOMINY

I'd often seen him rising there
When the flies were sailing down;
I deemed, some day, I'd hook him fair,
And tempt him from his guarded lair,
With " Greenwell " or " March Brown."

His home was by a willow-tree,
Where it hung close o'er the stream;
There oft I'd crouched on bended knee,
Casting a fly most daintily,
With art and skill supreme.

Again I sauntered forth to try
My wiles on that ancient trout—
I reached my goal, but to descry
A youth who'd hooked him, not with fly,
But worm, and dragged him out!

CHAPTER V

HANDICAPPED ANGLERS

ONE would naturally expect that the gentle and delicate art of fly-fishing would necessitate the angler's being in full possession of his limbs and senses. Good eyesight particularly would appear to be an essential.

Yet there have been many fishermen who have been expert at the sport notwithstanding the handicap of total loss of sight and other grave defect or disablement.

When I was but a callow youth I first experienced wonder—and pity too—at seeing an oldish man, who was without hands, fishing with the fly for trout in the River Crake, at Blawith, near where that river debouches from Lake Coniston.

I watched him throw his line dexterously; I saw him hook, and play, and land trout; I saw him take them off the hook and creel them; and I saw him, too, unhook small fish with gentle carefulness, so that the "infant prey" were unhurt, and put them back into the water.

This angler, I learned, was an example of what can be done by grit and determination under the most adverse circumstances. As a boy, he had worked in a factory, and, as the result of an accident, had lost both hands at the wrists. His career as an artisan was thus cut short; but a Good

Samaritan, who had faith in the lad's abilities, had helped him in such a way that he had been trained to become a school teacher. He taught the village school at the time I first saw him. He was also—as is, or was, usual in remote rural districts—parish clerk, and held sundry other useful and necessary offices appertaining to the communal life of a parish and village. It was a matter of wonderment to strangers to see him sitting below the pulpit o' Sundays, and turning over the leaves of the Prayer Book with his handless stumps and his lips, as he led the responses in a sonorous voice.

Of one-armed salmon-fishers I have met several. They have been, mostly, men who during an active military career have lost an arm in action. This has not deterred them from carrying on their angling afterwards. But, after all, salmon-fishing is not the delicate art that trout-fishing is; and, moreover, the one-armed men I have known as skilled anglers have been men of means, who could afford to keep a man in attendance to tie the flies on, row a boat, and gaff or net the fish. Yet it must require much practice, and the exercise of considerable judgment and skill, to cast a fly or bait with a salmon-rod with one arm only, and to play such heavy and vigorous fish when hooked. It is generally facilitated by the fisherman having the butt of the rod resting in a leathern socket, strapped round the waist.

Blind anglers would seem to miss the great delights the fisherman enjoys—such as the scenery and the wild life which are such notable features of our riversides; but even this grave and sad disability has not been enough to deter some men from the sport.

An outstanding case was that of the late Professor Fawcett, a noted Victorian statesman, who was taught to fish for salmon, when totally blind, by one of the fishermen to the Duke of Roxburghe. But here again was a case where a blind man had the benefit of being able to pay for a fisherman-attendant to advise and guide him.

A more wonderful case was that of the blind fisherman of St Boswells, who, without any attendant but his dog, would spend his summer evenings fishing for trout.

It is said that he was quite a master of the art, and as expert as any man possessed of full sight. He would wade into the river, and seemed to have an uncanny instinct which guided him from the dangerous depths and powerful currents. Not only could he put his fishing-gear together without assistance, but he made his own flies, and really excellent ones they were said to be. He had, too, a good reputation as a maker of first-class fishing-rods.

There was an army major I knew who suffered from that dire ailment *locomotor ataxy*, with gradually approaching total blindness. He had been a keen salmon-fisher for years, and did not give it up until he was rendered physically helpless. Another angler I knew of had a severe form of heart trouble, and, in spite of frequent painful attacks of his malady, when out fishing he was not to be deterred from the thrills and excitements of hooking and playing heavy salmon. But it was climbing a hill, when out with the guns after grouse, that was the immediate cause of his sudden demise.

Of a handicap being turned to advantage one

recalls the story, often told on Tweedside, of a certain " Old Timbertoes." A salmon-angler, lawfully pursuing his sport one chilly day in the early part of the season, observed an old fellow fishing a stream for trout. Although the water was bitterly cold, the old trout-fisher was devoid of any protective wading stockings, and the angler remarked to his boatman that surely it could not be good for him to be standing so long in the cold water without wearing waders.

" Oh! he's all right, sir," replied the boatman. " He has two wooden legs, and if you will watch him you will see he has a third, which he uses as a seat, as you would use a shooting-stick."

And sure enough the ancient was settled there in the water in comparative comfort and ease on his wooden tripod, successfully hooking trout, and quite oblivious of the fact that the water was distinctly cold and chilling.

AT DRYBURGH

THE TWEED AT DRYBURGH

[*page* 86

AT THE EILDON TREE

Here rade the lovely elfin queen,
    As Thomas lay by Eildon Tree;
And he is up on her milk-white steed,
    Tae ride to realms of Faery.

Betide him weal, betide him woe,
    Seven lang, lang years awa' was he;
For seven lang years was seen nae moe,
    By Ercildoune or Eildon Tree.

Syne Rymour Thomas freed was he
    Tae roam o'er Huntlybanks again;
Fu' stored wi' lear o' wizardry,
    Was gi'en him by the elfin queen.

Though Thomas wove a cunning spell
    Of gramerie o'er Tweed's fair vale,
He little recked, nor did foretell,
    Another wizard would prevail.

Yet had the Rymour never been
    Beneath the queen of Faery's spell,
The greatest wizard yet, I ween,
    Might ne'er have charmed the world so well.

CHAPTER VI

AT DRYBURGH

IF you will come with me to the Braeheads, the prominent bluff that is situated just behind the hamlet of Lessudden, you shall see one of the fairest scenes in the whole vale of Tweed, combining river, woodland and pasture in one composite picture.

Here the river makes a graceful sweep round an elbow of rich pastoral land, enfolding it in a tender embrace, and within that embrace are gathered the ruins of the ancient abbey of Dryburgh, guarded by noble trees of yew, and elm, and beech, fringed round by green pastures—verily an exquisite gem in a fair setting. And within the cloistered ruins rest two of Scotland's greatest men, whose names are writ amongst those of the immortals.

The impressive calm and charm of the scene, viewed from this point of vantage high above yet near to it, are calculated to move the emotions of the most prosaic among us, and to inspire us with thoughts above the sordid things of present-day existence.

Where else will you find so noble a scene of picturesque and peaceful beauty conjoined with such associations? To describe it with full justice would call for the poetic genius of a Wordsworth, or the author of *The Seasons*, since mere prose were too feeble and inadequate.

By Scotsmen the world over—and not by Scotsmen alone, be it added—the very name of Dryburgh Abbey is spoken with reverence, since within its sacred precincts the remains of Walter Scott, the great Wizard of the North, have reposed for more than a hundred years, amidst surroundings which have been peaceful and quiet beyond imagining.

Now there keeps him company one who was great in war, a soldier *sans peur et sans reproche*, one who served his country well at a time of dire need, and saved it from a ruthless and not always chivalrous foe. His country honoured him, and not the least of the many honours that came to him was the gift from his own countrymen which enabled his family to bestow his remains within Dryburgh's hallowed walls, where he may hear Tweed's song ever murmuring as the river rolls by through the ages coming.

To the angler, who may be attracted by the historic and literary associations of the surroundings where he pursues his quest of sport, there can be few more interesting fishing headquarters than the vicinity of Dryburgh, since the Tweed will here yield him a great variety of pool and stream and rippling shallow, a fair prospect of a well-filled creel, and scenery that is pleasing, varied, restful and refreshing to the mind and eye. Moreover, round about him he will find many scenes associated with history and tradition that will arouse his interest, and give him food for thought and contemplation in the intervals of his fishing, when the river may not be in order for sport.

The angler has already been introduced to the Braeheads, and has taken his first glimpse of the abbey across the water; but perhaps, before he commences his fishing, he may be desirous of spying out the land.

So let us, for a few moments, remove our gaze from the abbey, and look round.

In the near distance the Eildon Hills form a prominent landmark, their three peaks sharply defined against the sky, to remind us of the wizard Michael Scott, whose book of magic was sought by William of Deloraine from the ancient monk of St Mary's Aisle in Melrose, who, in handing it over to him, owned that despite his holy calling he had some unholy knowledge of the magician's craft:

> " And, warrior, I could say to thee
> The words that clove Eildon Hills in three,
> And bridled the Tweed with a curb of stone."

The whole of this countryside is saturated with legend and story. There was Thomas the Rhymer, of Ercildoune—just at the foot of the Black Hill, the summit of which you can see from here—who was whisked off by the Faery Queen on her milk-white steed when he met her at the Eildon Tree, by Huntlybank, just beyond the Bogle Burn, which crosses the road to Melrose. Thomas returned to earth, so goes the ancient tale, some years later, full learned in the arts and wiles of gramerie and wizardry, and endowed with the powers of a seer. To Thomas the Rhymer is ascribed the prediction that

> " Tide, tide, whate'er betide,
> There'll aye be Haigs in Bemersyde."

From where we stand we can see the hill on which is the historic keep of Bemersyde, presented with the surrounding lands to the most illustrious and famous of all the Haigs—the one who rests just down below us, so near to his last earthly home, which he loved so well. It had come to pass that, when the old race of Haigs seemed to be dying out, a Haig arose to fill the breach and fulfil the ancient prophecy.

As for the structure of Bemersyde House, it is like to endure for long years yet—at any rate, the early part of the house. Some years ago we surveyed the building in connection with some projected improvements, and in taking measurements for our purpose found that the walls of the original keep were composed of solid masonry ten feet thick.

On the breast of the rise up to Bemersyde you may see, excepting when the trees are in fullest foliage, a crude effigy of enormous size, erected by the eccentric Earl of Buchan, who once owned the surrounding lands, to " the peerless knight of Ellerslie," Sir William Wallace. 'Tis not a graceful monument, nor a thing of beauty. To many it is but an unsightly blot on the rural scene.

From Bemersyde Hill it is no great distance to Smailholm Tower, a somewhat bleakly-situated and lonely Border peel associated with the name of Sir Walter Scott, who, when a child, stayed with kinsfolk at Sandyknowe Farm, near by, so that his constitution might be braced and built up in the pure air of the hills. While there he assimilated the very spirit of the countryside, absorbing in his retentive mind the legends and ballad stories which were to influence him so greatly when he began to write. In his own words he

" . . . marvelled as the aged hind
With some strange tale bewitched his mind."

Not far away, to our right, is Mertoun House, where the Scotts of Harden, to which family Sir Walter's was kin—a family descended from that hardy mosstrooper and reiver Auld Wat of Harden —resided for many years. To anglers it is a house of interest, inasmuch as it was while a guest at Mertoun House that William Scrope wrote his *Days and Nights of Salmon Fishing on the Tweed*, a book which has come to be regarded as a classic work on angling for salmon, as indeed it deserves to be.

In the annals of fishing in the neighbourhood of Dryburgh there are many names of note, besides Scrope's.

There was the lowly cobbler John Younger, who dwelt by the green at Lessudden, and attracted to his modest workshop men of low and high degree to discuss many subjects besides fishing, although fishing was doubtless the main topic, and formed the excuse for opening the discussions. John was an expert wielder of the rod, and he was listened to as an authority on all that pertained to the sport.

A strange character was John Younger in some ways. A true lover of nature, somewhat of a poet —he wrote some charming verses and lectured on Robert Burns—yet he ridiculed the angler who would allow his mind to stray from the serious business in hand (to wit, the killing of salmon or trout), and to dwell on the glories of the riverside and the desire to wield the angle-wand to the glory of God, as exhorted to by the good Dame Berners and the devout old Izaak.

And yet, in the hungry years of the Corn Laws, when wheat was selling at one hundred-and-twenty-five shillings the quarter, and the quartern loaf was as high as two shillings, I make no doubt that the dour John had cause full many a time and oft to give thanks to the Maker of all good things for the rivers near at hand, from which he cozened many a good, wholesome meal, with his fishing - rod. Otherwise, he and his family would have had to be content with scantier and more simple fare. For has he not told us, in his own words, how, when he dwelt at Longnewton, he " flew to the Ale Water and fished for trout as much for his dinner as for amusement "?

Strange to say, in Dryburgh and its associations with the monkish life and ideals John took neither interest nor pleasure. To him the monks had been the enemies of the people, and had retarded rather than helped the advance of education and enlightenment amongst them. For the writings of Sir Walter Scott he had something very like contempt: he deemed them mere caricatures of Scottish life and manners.

Perhaps, after all, John's disdain of the manner in which Walton, and the earlier writer of *A Treatyse of Fysshynge wyth an Angle*, mingled piety and fishing was but a pose of his Radical mind. There is every reason to believe he was second to none in his love of wild nature and the beauties of the countryside where he was privileged to dwell and ply his fishing-wand.

There were other anglers of note, contemporaneous with Younger, who often sought the Dryburgh and Lessudden waters, and not the least of these was Stoddart, who has written of great catches of trout hereabouts. But Stoddart must surely have made a labour of his fishing, since he writes of commencing his day at Mertoun Cauld, and finishing as far up the river as the Monks' Ford, or even at the Gateheugh at Old Melrose—a long, long trail when equipped with all an angler's accoutrements, and laden, maybe, with a creel of fish ever growing in weight as he progressed. Possibly— nay, I should say probably—he skipped all but the choicest bits of water. He could not have fished it all carefully, even in a long summer's day.

Stoddart was an adept at fishing with the worm upstream on a summer day, when waters were low, and by this means he took great toll of the trout: creels of twenty and twenty-one pounds are amongst his records, and he naïvely adds that had he not curtailed his sport on one of these occasions, owing to an attack of lumbago, he could have doubled his catch with ease.

There was a kindred spirit with Stoddart in one William Henderson, erstwhile of Durham, who took delight in fishing at Dryburgh. He wrote a book about his experiences, and it is one of the most interesting and delightful of all fishing-books relating to sport on the Tweed, and its tributaries, since he gives us charming word-pictures of the anglers whom he met, professional and otherwise, and details of the sport he obtained in the various streams. He was claimed by Stoddart as one of his friends, and, in turn, he claimed to be the introducer of his particular and favourite method of fishing upstream with the worm. In his book he makes some very kindly allusions to John Younger, with whom he was " weel acquaint," and in whose workshop he spent many hours discussing fishing

95

affairs, as well as affairs of State. Henderson laments that John was such a Radical—from which we may deduce that they must have had some rare argumentative " cracks."

It was unfortunate that Stoddart and Younger had a disagreement. It was, after all, much ado about nothing—each accusing the other, in print, of poaching on the other's literary preserves. It would have been interesting to have heard the three of them—Younger, Stoddart and Henderson —talking about their angling experiences, as they were all skilled fishermen, observant of Nature in her varied moods, and students of human nature too. At least two of them were endowed with the poet's fine perception of what is delicate, tender and beautiful, while the third, if not himself a poet, was also fully capable of appreciating the fine things of art and life and wild nature in all their wondrous phases.

There was another fisherman, noted as a man of some character as he grew in years. He was a young man in Stoddart's time, and passed away in the late 1890's. Often have I chatted with him in his declining days. He had a little hut near the Suspension Bridge, where he sold flies for fishing, and such necessities of life as tobacco and cigarettes, filling in his time by fashioning various little articles to sell as souvenirs to tourists who visited the abbey.

Tom Fox had been custodian of the bridge at one time, and collected the tolls. He was always outspoken and fearless with his speech, and this attribute gave rise to some amusing stories.

There was one occasion on which a party of excursionists visited the abbey. They called themselves "pan-presbyterians," whatever that may denote. As they passed over the frail bridge some of them did their utmost, by jumping from side to side, to make it sway violently. Tom was watching them from the bank, and roared out to them to cease their fooling, for, if they didna—well, they micht be pan-presbyterians the noo, but they would soon be baptists.

On another occasion a party of young ministers called at his hut, and engaged him in conversation, trying to draw from him some of his quaint views on life and religion. Tom was no fool, and knew well that there was a vein of insincerity running through the talk. In other words, the young ministers, but newly fledged from the schools, and full of intellectual pride or conceit, were bent on making fun of the old man. But he was quite ready for them.

" Look ye here," he said. " D'ye see yon sign-post at the cross-roads? It's aye pointing the road, but it never gangs itsel'. Some o' ye meenisters are just like that: aye pointing the road to heaven; but how many o' ye gang there? "

Tom was one of those rare men who can charm the wild birds from the trees. He would whistle them down, and they would expectantly hop around him as he fed them. There seemed to be an understanding between him and the wild creatures as he chattered away to them. But I never heard of his attempting to emulate the holy St Francis of Assisi by preaching to the birds. Tom's feathered friends flocked to him for the sake of the crumbs he gave them, and looked not for spiritual comfortings.

To recall Tom Fox and his times—when the majority of the pilgrims to the abbey and Sir Walter's tomb came by way of the St Boswells road to the bridge-end, and passed over the bridge, then decorously on foot down the sylvan peaceful lanes to the old ruin—serves to remind us of the different conditions prevailing now.

Before the Great War, and before the coming of the motor-car, the abbey was not so easily accessible as now, although there was a fairly constant stream of visitors who paid respectful homage to Sir Walter's memory, and the peace and quiet of the countryside did not suffer.

Quel, nous avons changé tout cela! as Sir Walter himself has quoted.

The approach to the abbey knows peace no more. The sweet old-time charm and calm are sullied, and have given way to the hoot of the motor-horn and the cries of itinerant vendors of trifles. The smell of noxious gases engendered by petrol engines taints the air, where erstwhile the sweet perfume of the hawthorn was predominant, in its due time. Ultra-modern pseudo-Japanese tea-gardens mar the pastoral beauty of the scene, with their multicoloured-umbrella shades flaunting over an array of small tables. Even on the Sabbath day great stir and commotion reigns, as if the people were gathered to make a post-war holiday—as indeed many of them are—rather than to make a reverent pilgrimage of homage to the memory of the illustrious dead.

> " Was ne'er in Scotland heard or seen
> Sic dancing and deray;
> Nowther at Falkland on the green,
> Nor Peebles at the play."

Yes, alas! times have changed, and not for the better, as some think.

But if on the highways—and even the byways—
there is much stir and ado, down by the riverside
nothing disturbs the peace of the fisherman. Here
he may ply his rod by day, or in the hushed quiet
of the summer evening hours, without annoyance
or hindrance from anything more noisy than the
waterfowl, or the birds in the woodlands, or the
lowing kine or bleating sheep in the pastures.

From Mertoun Bridge to the Monks' Ford the
angler may find many a pool and many a stream
from which he may at any time lure a good trout,
in spring and summer. I have recollections of
baskets weighing eight pounds each, containing
twelve trout and fourteen trout respectively, caught
in a few hours on April days with the fly—a goodly
average weight of about three-quarters of a pound
each; and I recall taking a basket of over twelve
pounds, including two trout of about two pounds
each, on a cold and stormy day, also in the month
of April.

There are memories of summer evenings and
summer nights which are pleasant to muse upon,
when success compensated the angler for the loss
of his beauty sleep, and oftentimes I have been so
fortunate as to creel heavy fish on summer nights.

The Suspension Bridge at Dryburgh is thrown
across a very fine pool, and if you stand thereon
and look upstream you get a good view of a nice
stretch of angling water. On the left is a high
scaur, along the base of which a daring angler may
scramble, if his nerve is good, and get many a game
and sportive fish. A little higher upstream the
Bowden Burn enters the main river, and when the
river is low in summer you will find its bed, opposite

the Burnfoot, to be strewn with boulders, behind which the trout rest. They come up in the evening from the Bridge Pool, and resort to the little streams and pot-holes formed by these rocks, and many a lusty trout is caught hereabouts in the summer nights. I have a vivid memory of taking a lively three-pounder here on the stroke of midnight at the beginning of June.

And so we could continue to write of trouting days and nights spent in the neighbourhood of Dryburgh. To the angler, each angling day is a different and a new experience, with its infinite variety of incidents; but to write of them were to make tedious repetition to the reader. To the angler who already knows the district it needs no recommendation; he will go back there whenever opportunity affords, as a salmon homes to its native river. To the fisherman who has not yet cast his lines in these pleasant places we can only say that he has a delightful excursion and experience to look forward to.

LUCKLESS DAYS AND NIGHTS OF TROUT-FISHING

"WAN WATER FROM THE BORDER HILLS"

[page 102

CHAPTER VII

LUCKLESS DAYS AND NIGHTS OF TROUT-FISHING

THE enthusiastic fisherman who dwells in some delectable spot, centrally situated within almost walking distance of half-a-score of trouting rivers and rivulets, is often envied by the angler who dwells in some town distant from such delights.

There are two sides to this question, if our hypothetic anglers have to earn their living where they dwell. The first-mentioned angler, although envied by the town-dweller, cannot always pick his days for an outing on river or burn. If he could, the chances are that he would go a-fishing only when the water was just right, when the wind was in the right quarter and the sky nicely clouded, with the atmosphere moist and balmy. In practice it does not quite work out like that.

There was a time when I was happily situated: a noble river almost within a stone's-throw of my door, and many lovely " waters " within an hour's walk or drive—I may mention that it was before the days of motor-bicycles and cars—but I had my daily work to perform, and duty had to come first, although perhaps I was guilty, on occasion, of going a-fishing when duty should have claimed me.

It often happened that I was favoured with grants of leave to fish private waters, waters on which it was indeed a coveted privilege to throw a line. Of necessity, these privileges were dated, and one had to make the best of the opportunity given. It was not always a good fishing day that one got— such days cannot be foretold when fixing a future date—and it sometimes turned out that the long-looked-for day was literally a wash-out. These were the luckless days; and yet, if they led to no entry in the diary of fish caught, one cannot look back down the years without recalling something of them with a quiet smile of pleasure.

There was that day I had been looking forward to on the Leader, on a water where usually one creeled some nice lots of trout, trout with almost as much colouring as a perch, lovely fish, and the best fighters, for their size, I ever caught.

The time was early May. The day was warm, slightly cloudy at the start, and heavier clouds blowing up with a soft breeze from the south-west presaging rain to come. The rain came all right. It came in torrents as I reached the river.

I fled to a rustic thatched summer-house for shelter, or I should have been drenched through, and I sat there for some hours, with the river below rising rapidly, until it became a raging torrent of seething and boiling red mud. I never saw Leader rise so quickly.

Of course fishing was hopeless. My permit was restricted to fly-fishing; but no kind of lure would have been of use in that roaring flood. So I sat on, studying the woodland scene within my purview, watching such birds as dared venture from the protective shelter of the trees not yet in full leaf, and listening to their plaintive pipings. They would get plenty of food when the deluge ceased, but in the meantime they seemed to be lamenting the scarcity of grubs and insects on the tree branches where they were pent by the rainstorm. Now and then a weasel would pop its head out of the lush undergrowth of bracken and fern, as it made its way down some more or less sheltered hunting track, or a water-vole could be seen scurrying along the margin of the stream, washed out of its home in all likelihood. On the branch of a willow overhanging the river perched a disconsolate-looking kingfisher, its gleaming coat of sapphire-blue and rosy-tinted breast showing distinctively amid the tender greenery of the willows' foliage. It was not altogether unpleasant in that thatched hut, in the heart of the woods near to nature, rain pattering on and pouring from the trees, and the river singing its stormy flood-song down below. From a fishing point of view it was a luckless day.

There was that other day, on the same river, when two of us spent the longest fishing day I ever had, and caught nothing.

It was midsummer, and there was a drought. Before we started off we knew it would probably be hopeless for fishing. Again we were restricted to fly only.

We left home about one o'clock in the morning, it being our intention to try the pools and the fringes of the streams in the grey of the dawning. Had we been clear-water worm-fishing we should probably have done well. Fly-fishing so early in the day was an experiment.

As we intended to have a long day we had provisioned ourselves accordingly, and included a very large bottle of cold tea, which I had packed into my capacious creel. It was rough going up the river-bed, and there were many rocky places to climb over. In clambering over a large rock I made a false step, and had to jump to save myself from a fall. Somehow my basket came unfastened, and the bottle of tea fell to the stony river-bed with a crash. That was a luckless beginning; and we had not yet put up our rods! We had carried the tea the best part of four miles, and we had a long dry day before us.

We fished up the river most carefully, searching out all the little pot-holes and shaded places, casting our flies as near as we dared into the hollows where the banks overhung a sure haunt of trout. It was of no avail. Not a fin seemed to be stirring, and never a silvery gleam in the clear water showed to hearten us.

We tried our flies wet, throwing up the water and across, and sinking them where there was any depth of water. We essayed the dry-fly method. It was no use; there seemed to be no life in the water. Moreover, there was no appearance of the natural fly to be seen. We were simply nonplussed. From past experience we had the right flies for the river, but for once they did not attract the trout.

The day wore on, the midsummer noonday sun shone perpendicularly on our heads, and the heat was oppressive. Before the sun rose high in the heavens we were mostly in the shade, for the river runs in a deep glade, between well-wooded banks which gave ample shelter for the angler.

However, we decided to rest, and have our midday lunch. So we hied to a pleasingly cool spot beneath towering fir-trees, and sat there for a while. We were tired. The heat made us drowsy, and I confess we had a nap. Anyway, it was no use fishing. We faintly hoped there might be some sort of a rise in the late afternoon or evening.

So when the sun began to move round behind the woods we set forth again, in sheer desperation, always hoping we should yet see the trout rising. It was not to be. We kept on through the late afternoon and evening. We waited on until the usual time for the evening rise, and took care to be near the full deep pools for the expected event. There was no evening rise.

Determined not to be beaten, we stayed on after sunset, and did some night fishing; but not even in the half-light of the northern summer night did we see any rings made by rising fish, or hear that cheerful plash or *plop!* which indicates to the fisherman that trout are feeding.

Two very tired young men reached home just after midnight. They had been out over twenty-three hours. They had used all the art they knew in their efforts to catch trout with fly, in a well-stocked water, on a broiling day in June. Yet not a single fish had they caught between them, nor had they seen one. They were not novices, or inexpert at the sport.

Many inexplicable happenings occur in fishing, but this that I have attempted to describe was the most disconcerting day that ever I experienced, and, incidentally, it was the longest day I ever put in at trout-fishing with the fly.

.   .   .   .

As a contrast to what I have written above, there was the occasion when the two of us spent a night fishing a very famous water of the Tweed, and came home with clean creels.

If one is prepared to lose one's sleep and fish all through a summer night, on a good water, it is very rarely indeed that no sport is met with. There are always trout cruising about—some of them real big ones—during summer nights, picking up odd moths and sedge-flies. So it is a very poor night that does not yield the fisherman some sport with heavy trout.

Our expectations ran high, for the water on which we were to fish held big trout, and lots of them. We had a short train journey, and had to cross a ferry to reach our starting-point, but we were on the water and fishing by about seven in the evening.

The water was at summer-level, but in fair order, so we hoped to pick up a trout or two before the evening rise, which occurred usually about ten o'clock.

Up to ten o'clock we had caught nothing, seen nothing, risen nothing. We paused, waiting for that phenomenon known as the evening rise. Never a dimple showed on the quietest pools. So we fished on and on into the night, but it was hopeless.

About midnight it became so dark that we had to desist, so we decided to rest for a time. We had seen a cave near by, and we went into it, curled ourselves up for a nap, and tried to sleep. But it was too eerie in there. Thousands of bats flitted in and out, uttering their faint yet weird squeaks, and ever and anon brushing our faces with their wings.

So we soon got out of that, and sauntered about until there was a faint glimmer of light showing in the sky.

We resumed our fishing, and continued until about six in the morning. Neither of us had seen or felt a fish, and our creels were empty. We could not account for it—just one of those luckless occasions which every angler, skilled or not, experiences sooner or later, when he begins to think he is losing his cunning, or that he has been making some egregious blunder in his methods. Fortunately he does not lose heart altogether, and perhaps the next time he goes out with rod and creel he may come back laden with the spoils of the chase.

There are, of course, days when the fisherman is out of luck in little things which annoy the more as being the result of want of care. These hardly come within the scope of my subject, and are in another category. Few anglers of long experience but what have known the chagrin of arriving at the fishing-ground to find that a favourite reel and line have been left at home, or that the fly-book is in need of replenishing, or even missing. Then, again, in absentminded zeal one may hook something behind when casting, and when swinging the cast forward snap the rod-top in consequence. Lucky fisherman if he is provided with a spare top. I have had friends borrow a rod—" just for a cast or two "—and walk off with it, carrying it at the trail point first, with the inevitable result of running it against a fence or tree and smashing it. Who amongst us has not known that kindly disposed but over-zealous helper who would insist on netting your best fish of the day for you, and making a mess of it, to your hardly suppressed anger when the fish got away. Keen anglers, too, sometimes make a false step when wading, and get an unwelcome dip. These little annoyances are, however, all in the game, and I would not include them as luckless days.

When I come to think of it, one of the most luckless days I ever knew was that glorious spring day when, not having much time to spare, and knowing I was short of the right type of fly, I rushed into a little shop where flies were sold as a sideline, and hurriedly bought what I thought would be a sufficiency. I knew I was taking a risk, as the old man who kept the shop was not to be relied on for keeping sound stuff.

However, I got my flies, tramped off to the river, and when I got there saw that the trout were already rising to the Blue Dun. I quickly fixed up rod and line, and attached some of my new flies. No sooner was my first cast on the water than up lunged a great trout and took the tail fly, but as soon as I put on a little pressure the fly broke away. In less than half-an-hour this happened quite a dozen times, and every time it was a good fish. I always reckoned the average weight of trout taken from this particular pool when the rise was good was very nearly a pound.

At last it occurred to me that either I was very clumsy or there was something wrong with the gut on which the flies were tied. So I tested the flies I had remaining, to find that the gut was as rotten as scorched cotton thread.

Verbum sat sapienti!

MIDSUMMER NIGHTS

THE MAYFLY

The Invitation

The Mayfly's up, and hatching free,
Come, leave behind your cares and toils!
For trout are rising, mad with glee—
The Mayfly's up, and hatching free,
Let's hie us to the stream, or we
May miss our chance to share the spoils—
The Mayfly's up, and hatching free,
Come, leave behind your cares and toils!

The Reply

The Mayfly's over—tell the Club
There's nothing moving now but chub!

CHAPTER VIII

MIDSUMMER NIGHTS

SHOULD you, some fine morning in June or July, take a fancy to be up early to see the sun rise over the hills in all his fresh glory, and to enjoy the wondrous spectacle of the mists rolling down the valleys, to melt away under the influence of its warming rays, you may chance to meet a fisherman returning with rod and creel from the river. You must be stirring betimes to see him, for the northern midsummer night is brief, and day dawns about two of the clock; although, indeed, these nights are never really dark, and when we have fair weather—free from cloud—consist but of grey twilight.

Our fisherman has, maybe, been out since the fore-part of the previous evening, in time for the rise of trout that may almost always be expected about sunset; but that is not what is understood by "night fishing" proper. After the evening rise there comes another phase. Then the fisherman removes his fine casting line, replacing it with a stronger one. He uses larger patterns of flies, too, for now he has hopes of capturing some of the big trout which leave the deep runs and pools, where they have been feeding on the bottom, and resort to the shallower places and backwaters, or to the surface of the stilly deeps close in to the river bank, steadily picking out the night sedge-flies and moths, which a keen eye can see fluttering on the water or floating placidly down.

There is enchantment and a subtle charm about the river these warm summer nights. Save for the diapason note of the river flowing over the rocks and swirling round the bend, where it beats against the foot of the scaur, there is little sound or movement anywhere. There is restful peace and silence. The birds ceased their merry songs at set of sun, and are seeking respite from their daily exertions in the branches of the trees hard by, until the dawn comes. The owl is calling his mournful note occasionally in the distant wood, and a querulous " caw " may be heard, now and again, from a restive rook disturbed in the swaying branches by the gentle breeze which moves in the higher stratum of air, albeit there is not a zephyr down below at the water-level. All else is hushed.

Not infrequently an otter may be seen swimming a pool in search of a victim, and, as the angler plies his rod quietly, the marauder may come up quite close to him, breaking the surface with his round muzzle almost at the feet of the fisherman. Both angler and otter are after trout, but the amphibian soon senses the presence of his enemy man, and dives below, to come up again at a safe distance.

An amusing incident here comes to my mind. The Professor and I were out fishing one warm June night, and I had noticed that my companion was very intent at the edge of a quiet pool, whipping away with his fly persistently, but without reward, and never a whir from the reel telling of fish being run. I was but twenty yards higher up the water, and he called me to come down. I reeled up and went, when he explained that he had been casting for quite a long time at an "enormous trout" which he avowed was steadily rising about five or six yards out.

As he had so far failed to induce it to rise to his fly, he suggested I might have better fortune. So I took his place, and essayed a cast or two, when, to my amusement and the Professor's disgust and chagrin, the " big trout " turned out to be a young otter. It, too, was evidently intent on sport in the deep pool, and came up at intervals in almost the same spot for a breath of air. We thereupon changed our quarters, for where the otter hunts or disports itself is no place to expect trout to rise to the fly.

Night fishing is not without adventure, and the unexpected often happens. Once, in my eagerness, I was constrained to wade more than half-way across towards a pool that lurked in a bend of the river where I was fishing, for I knew there were good trout there if I could only reach them.

The river-bed was familiar to me, and the water was low, so there was really little risk in wading in the semi-darkness. Several trout were rising, my attention being wholly concentrated on them, when suddenly two bright flashes blazed out just in front of me, and simultaneously the air was rent with the loud reports of a right and left from a sporting gun. It seemed to me that the shots were aimed in my direction, and I fear my language was not quite polite. The explanation was that the gamekeeper on the estate was crouching on the river bank in wait for otters appearing in the pool that I was fishing. He said that he had seen two young ones, and had fired at them. My opinion at the time was that it was a senseless thing to do in the dark, as he could not have recovered the animals if he had killed them, nor would their pelts, which he said he wanted, have been very good, as it was midsummer. However, he expressed his regrets for startling me, saying that I had not been in any danger, as he knew I was fishing there. At least I think he might have warned me.

There was a more amusing, though none the less startling, adventure on another occasion. If I had been more timid or imaginative I could have made a blood-curdling ghost-story out of it.

As I came quietly down the waterside—it was long past the witching hour of midnight—peering out for the sign of a rising trout, my career was abruptly brought to a halt.

There was suddenly a loud splashing in the backwater just below me, a shrill screaming and whistling noise filled the air, which seemed to be peopled with winged demons whose pennons almost brushed my face as they wafted on their demoniac way. It was so unexpected that my hair, for a second or two, took on a tendency to raise my " bonnet " from my head, and a shiver went down my spine! But the fuss was much ado about nothing. Unaware of their proximity I had almost stepped on to a patriarchal wild drake and his spouse, who had taken up their quarters for the night, with their brood of half-grown flappers.

The noise a family of this description can make when disturbed, all else being hushed at dead of night, is appalling, and must be heard in the circumstances I have attempted to describe to be fully appreciated.

The best nights for fishing are those when the sky is shaded with a screen of dull cloud, not too dense, for then the river seems to reflect all objects from its surface, and every movement and ripple is easily seen by a keen-sighted angler. On such a night you may find trout rising steadily, and in a humour for taking your artificial flies.

Heavy thundery nights are of little use unless you wish to catch eels, and it is a curious phenomenon that when the air is heavy with thunder eels seem to come to the surface and will take a fly. This I have observed on more than one occasion. If the water is covered with white rolling mist—a " *haar* " or " rook " as the Border angler calls it—you may as well pack up your rod and seek repose.

For night fishing the angler will need a stronger casting line than that he would use earlier in the evening, and larger flies. It is not advisable to use more than two flies at the same time on a night cast, and I have found it an advantage, on a night that has been dark, to use one fly only. The more flies you have on your line the more chances you have of entanglement, resulting in wasted time and the loss of that placid and even temper which the angler should never lose. It is always a wise thing to do, also, to examine frequently the barbs of your hooks. Unwittingly one may hit a rock on the bank behind when casting, and the finely tempered steel of the hook may snap. I have risen great trout, and lost them, at night, to find that they have risen to a barbless hook, much to my disgust.

For flies, the Woodcock and Harelug, Corncrake, Grey Drake, and Teal and Red patterns will be found useful, and the angler can add to these at his discretion, according to local conditions.

There is little occasion to wade when night fishing, for trout leave the deep holes and pools and strong-running streams when the sun sets, and resort to the shallows and the fringes of the river, close in to the reeds and river-edge growths of vegetation, where they find an abundance of insect life moving.

If you would have proof of this, wade slowly down a stretch of rippling water, fringing deep streams and pools, in the grey of the dawn, keeping well away from the river bank, and you will sense the presence of innumerable trout, of unbelievable size, with their back-fins almost out of the water. Then, as you disturb their quietude, they will turn tail and scutter past you to the safer deeps whence they came, making brave waves on the surface as they go, and such a splashing as makes the angler wonder what sort of fight they would make if hooked on light tackle. I have seen them in hundreds thus, congregated on the shallows; and after an evening and night out on the water when my efforts to creel a few have been poorly rewarded, making me think that there were few fish there, the ocular proof of an abundant stock of fish was always heartening, and an incitement to try again, when perhaps circumstances would be more propitious and result in the filling of a creel.

The doubt may occur whether night fishing is fair and sportsmanlike, and whether the angler is taking a mean advantage of the trout by seeking their destruction when they are, in a sense, somewhat off their guard. After all, trout are very wary and suspicious even at night, and it is no duffer's game to catch them then, for they seem to know by instinct that the least movement of the riverside reeds portends danger, and that where there is an unusual ripple there is an enemy lurking. There are, it is true, no shadows to betray the presence of the angler or his rod, but trout that lie close in to the bank seem to have an uncanny intuition of the presence of danger, and move out of harm's way.

There is one aspect of night fishing which deserves consideration. It is at night that the angler will kill heavy trout, and the river is well rid of the great fellows, the habits of many of them being cannibalistic in a high degree. Ugly trout, some of these, that raven on their weaker brethren, and to that extent spoil the fishing and injure the stock. For a cannibal trout of four or five or more pounds is almost as great an enemy to a trout-fishery as a jack or pike, and he is better out of the way. They may be caught by spinning a minnow in a floodwater that is waning, it is true; but a greater proportion of them fall victims to the fly during the midsummer nights. And this is one of the great fascinations of night fishing, for sooner or later you will capture a real big one, which will be as a milestone on your angling way through life.

While the hope and expectation of capturing big trout form part of the pleasure of night fishing, the smaller ones are not to be despised. Indeed, if you can creel a dozen, or a dozen and a half or so, of average-sized fish, you have a basket which will be a delight, for at this time of the year they are plump and well-fed, and give great sport ere they are netted or drawn up the shingle. They will average over half-a-pound in weight, and you are likely to have one or two pounders among them—and a pound trout on a northern river is no mean capture. Many a trout from a pound weight up to three pounds or so have I creeled at night, but never a heavier one, although I have known of many others up to six pounds caught by other anglers.

However, while night fishing has its pleasing aspects, it is not a sport for any but the hardy, the active and the keen-eyed. It is so easy in the semi-darkness to stumble over an unseen projecting rock or a derelict tree-stump. A false cast, when one's eye cannot follow the fall of the fly and line with any great certainty, so often results in an entanglement or being hooked on a snag or tree branch, or even on a tall reed by the riverside, and the lack of light to enable the angler to put things to rights again calls for the exercise of all his store of patience.

Yet, with all its drawbacks, a night out on the river is an experience worth while undergoing, and if the basket be but a light one—and it often is—there is always something to interest the fisherman. And if your river be in a wooded country it is worth while having lost some hours of sleep to be there at dawn, to hear the first tentative twitterings of the army of unseen birds, awaking as the first grey gleams come over the hills, and the mighty burst of song which almost immediately follows, when all the woodlands and the riverside seem alive with feathered songsters, each singing his loudest notes in joy that the day has again begun in which to take delight of life.

If the angler be wise, now is the time for him to take down his rod, and seek his couch for a few hours' repose, with the sweet music of nature still ringing in his ears, to bring refreshing peace.

OF RIVERSIDE WILDINGS:

OF THE BIRDS
OF THE BEASTS
AND THE FLORA

NESTING TIME

Blue skies above, and the laverock lilting:
Rooks in the tree-tops, noisy at their nesting;
Buds—swollen wine-red—on the elms are bursting;
    And the lintie sings, love-lorn.

Joyful in the hedgerows birds pipe in chorus—
" Gone is Winter dreary, Summer is before us;
Sweet ! we cannot wait, here we'll embower us,
    And weave our nest in the thorn."

Blue are the skies, while Mother Earth is greening;
Lovers stroll adown the lane, each to other leaning—
" Sweetheart ! 'tis mating time: hear how birds are singing,
    Of love's sweetest hopes new-born ! "

CHAPTER IX

OF RIVERSIDE WILDINGS

OF THE BIRDS:

WHAT a wealth of rapture and enjoyment the observant fisherman may reap as he contemplates nature by a riverside, or strolls down the fisherman's track on his way thither. There may be some fishermen to whom the primrose by the river's brim is but a yellow primrose and nothing more; or who go a-fishing in the spirit of the butcher who slays a bullock or a sheep, and are merely imbued with a desire for slaughter. But such men are not true disciples of the good Father Izaak, and one would fain think they are few and far between.

Wild nature is always entrancingly fascinating to most anglers, and, while I may candidly confess that I never forget, when I go a-fishing, that I am out for the purpose of catching fish, and use my uttermost skill and craft to that end, yet there are times when some aspect of nature and wild life will distract my attention and cause me to turn aside from my main purpose.

I must have been very young indeed when I first began to take an interest in the glories of creation, and the wild life around our countryside.

Amongst my earliest recollections are memories of finding a bird's nest in a woodland coppice into which I had strayed. How wonderfully fashioned it was, to my young mind: how cunningly rounded and smoothed inside, and the whole so artfully hidden in a hawthorn. There were pale sky-blue eggs in it, and I was spellbound and almost awed at the wondrous beauty and delicacy they exhibited. With quivering delight I told my old grandfather of my discovery, and he said I must have found a throstle's nest.

I was to learn later that the " throstle " was the thrush, or the mavis of the poets.

This was the beginning of much nature lore I learned from the old man. A blackbird to him was always a " black ouzel," as distinguished from the water-ouzel, that dapper bird with the white waist-coat which the angler will so often see flirting on a stone, and admiring himself in a mirroring pool of the stream. I was told much of the habits of the various birds; of where they usually built their nests, and how to find them, and the description of nest each made, and the colour of its eggs. Above all else, it was instilled into me that I was to refrain from cruelty when bird's-nesting; never to despoil a nest, since the song-birds, especially, apart from their beauty, gave us such pleasure with their carolling morning and evening as they sang to their mates sitting in their nests. Then, again, my grand-father held that most birds had their practical value on the farm, as they were always picking up grubs and worms and many a crawling pest which harmed the crops.

At that very early period of my life we lived in an old country house that had at one time been a farmhouse, and we were the fortunate possessors of an ancient orchard, where the wild birds made sanctuary. Many a nest of thrush and wren, linnet and robin, chaffinch, bullfinch and hedgesparrow, and others, did I find. The sitting birds would soon get to know I meant them no harm; and when I would peep through the branches and twigs, to see how they were doing, the bird on the nest would cock its eye and look up at me, as if to let me know that things were going on very nicely, thank you.

Schoolfellows of mine there were who "collected" birds' eggs, and they deemed it no shame or crime to harry a nest. Some, more merciful than others, would take but one or two eggs from a clutch; others would take all. Some were so wantonly or thoughtlessly cruel that they would take nest as well, or break it down. Whenever I found a nest I took good care not to let these fellows see me go near it, for it was a real agony to me to see such heartless cruelty.

What I learned of birds and their nests in my boyhood's days has ever been a delight to me as I grew older; and whenever I have made a fishing excursion the joy and pleasure of it have been augmented if I could find a nest by the river, or see a bird that is rarely seen by men who do not fish. Many a bird it is a pleasure to watch is seen by anglers who keep their eyes open at the waterside.

What a delight, for example, it is to see the kingfisher scudding beneath the willows, when the sunlight flickers through the branches. To me it seems like a flash of emerald-green, as it passes beneath the reflecting greenery of the drooping boughs; but others will have it that the bird's colouring is of sapphire-blue. The blue is maybe the reflex of the blue zenith: in French folklore they have the pretty story that when Noah set the birds free from the Ark it was the kingfisher who got away first, and was privileged to dye his breast with the rose-red rays of the setting sun, and to carry on his back for all time the reflection of the azure sky. But the robin and the bullfinch must surely have been there also when the sun was setting rosy red!

Then there is the stately heron, standing immovably on the fringe of a forest of reeds by the marge of the stream or mere, waiting so patiently until an unwary fish, be it trout or eel, shall swim within reach of his long and merciless beak, when its rapid thrust into the waters reveals how watchful the bird has been, in spite of its apparent immobility. The heron will attack small animals as well as fish, such as water-voles and frogs, and he is an interesting bird to watch from a hidden point of vantage. But should you openly approach the heron he will soon rise into the air, in that seemingly slow and lazy way he has, although you will be astonished at the rapidity of his flight, as his great spread of wing carries him away from harm, and over the tree-tops, to his eyrie.

Why is the heron the pet aversion of the crow family? Oftentimes have I observed a solitary heron in full flight, chivied and chased by numbers of crows, who emitted raucous noises of displeasure, and every now and then made a fierce and spiteful dart at the bigger and clumsier bird.

Of the wild duck that nests in some secluded and hidden spot on the river bank, or on an islet, and

tries to induce you to follow her as she makes
pretence of a lame wing and would lead you away
from her nest; of moorhen and dabchick, dodging
in and out of the reeds and rushes; of the lapwing
or " peewit " you may alarm as you take a short
cut across the marshy land towards the river, and
who also will try to draw your attention and guide
you, if you will follow, away from her precious nest
and eggs; of the partridge that behaves very much
as does the wild duck if you approach too near her
nest in brooding time, when, in order to shorten
your journey to the river, you climb over the whin-
covered knoll which slopes to the south and catches
most of the sunshine—of all these, and many more,
the angler who keeps his eyes looking around him,
as he passes to and from his fishing, may take his
delight in observing, and in storing his memory
with food for pleasant reflection when he may be
far from scenes of country life, or the river be in the
grip of icy winter.

What a gladsome thing it is, too, to hear the
cuckoo's note for the first time in the spring,
proclaiming that the " Summer is icumen in," and
prophetic of the sunnier, warmer days to come.

In the tree-tops the wood-pigeon croons his
amorous song, making a noisy clatter of wings as
he takes flight to his feeding-grounds in search of
food for the young and hungry brood. And as the
fisherman reels up his line in the evening, preparatory to returning home, a flock of noisy rooks
may be heard flying overhead on their way to the
rookery. A pheasant is going fussily to roost in a
close-by fir-tree, and in the wood is heard the hoot
of an owl, to herald the early approach of night.

133

OF THE BEASTS:

Should an angler be fishing in the daytime he will not, in this island of ours, see a great deal of our wild mammals in the height of the fishing season. Sometimes, when passing a coppice, or a thickset hedge, or a stone dyke, he may catch a glimpse of the weasel or the stoat, slithering through the undergrowth in a snakelike fashion, on the track, very likely, of a rabbit, which, if the fisherman's hearing is acute, he may hear squealing in its death throes when he is quite a distance away. The weasel is a lithe and graceful creature, but I own I like him not. Never have I encountered more than two at a time, although I have read of a pack of twenty or so hunting with noses to the ground, tracking down a party of young boys. But my own experience of the creature is that, although he will show his sharp teeth with a snarl at you, if you disturb him, he will not attack you.

Most of our wild animals are creatures of the night, and are oftenest met with late in the evening as they leave their lairs for the hunting-grounds, or in the early morning as they return home from the hunt. But I recall, one early autumn afternoon, traversing the edge of a small glen, at the bottom of which there was a patch of green turf adjacent to a number of large trees, beyond which was the fringe of a pheasant cover. The sun was bright, and its rays fell on the turf, where I saw the entertaining sight of an old vixen lying sunning herself, with her cubs gambolling about her like young puppy dogs, and the fox joining in the play as if he enjoyed it. The cubs were well grown, and I make no doubt that they made sport for the hounds a few months later on, for this was in a hunting country. I watched them for a time, and they all soon settled down quietly.

But the old fox sat up on his haunches with his ears cocked as if listening. Then he crept away from the others and went a few yards up the glen, where I saw him hide crouching behind the bole of an elm, and following the direction of his gaze I saw a brace of pheasants feeding placidly and oblivious of danger about twenty yards away, and Reynard the fox was deliberately stalking them. He did not get them, however, since I threw a stone down the glen and disturbed the birds, which flew to safety, for a time at least.

Frequently have I met a fox in the late evening or early morn when I have been out with a fishing-rod. I recall one moonlit night sensing the presence of a prowler by the strong smell, as I crossed a ride in the wood. So I looked about, and noticed a pair of green eyes peering from behind a tree. I advanced towards them, and as I did so the eyes receded round the tree. He played this game for a little while, and then made a sudden bound aside, and loped off in the moonlight, like a black shadow.

I have more than once interrupted a fox, just about dawn, lying in wait near a rabbit warren. The rabbits of course would leave their burrows at daybreak, to feed on the dew-laden herbage near by, and this would be the fox's opportunity, an opportunity of which he had doubtless taken many an advantage.

In the grey twilight of a midsummer night I was once a witness of an amusing scene. I had been fishing until after midnight, and was taking a short cut across a haugh on my way towards home. The haugh was very hummocky, due partly to the large number of moles which dwelt there having thrown up the soil repeatedly, and as I was avoiding one unusually large mound I thought it seemed to be moving. A close examination, however, revealed that there were seven or eight hedgehogs on it, indulging in a sort of " King of the castle " game.

It was very funny. One or two of the prickly " urchins " would take up a position on the peak of the mound, and, as if on a given signal, the others would charge up the hill and endeavour to dislodge the " kings," who, on their part, charged down at the attackers. They seemed to be having great fun, and emitted what were evidently squeaks of delight, as one or two at a time could be seen rolling down the hill like balls.

The agility and speed they displayed as they ran up the mound was astonishing, and surprising in such short-legged little animals, and when they rolled down all curled up in a ball it was a curious sight to see how quickly they could resume their normal position and dash up the hill again on their four legs. They appeared quite oblivious of my presence, so intent were they on their sport, and I was a spectator for quite a long time. How long they kept it up I do not know, as I left them still playing their game.

Of all the wild creatures that the angler meets during his excursions perhaps the otter is the most interesting, although the fisherman regards this picturesque creature with somewhat mixed feelings. There is no doubt that the otter takes fish, and equally true is it that he will scare all the salmon from a pool in one night. But I doubt if, after all, he does a very great deal of damage to the fisheries.

I have watched the otter swimming about the pools both in daylight and after sundown, and have come to the conclusion that he does not kill a great many fish.

Early one evening, long before sundown, I observed the biggest otter I have ever seen—he must have been very nearly four feet from his snout to the end of his broad tail. The animal was in some quiet-running water, close in to the river bank, with the sun shining directly upon him, so that, from a high bank, I could see his every movement. The otter was quite unaware of my proximity. He was evidently hunting for food, and I judged, from the way he nosed into the river bank and the river channel, he was looking for eels or water-voles. During the time I kept him in view, however, he did not catch anything.

Often when fishing at night I have seen otters, alone or with their young, more often than not seeming to be bent on playful sporting, diving and gliding about the waters, and I never saw one actually with a trout or salmon, although I did once find a fish which had apparently been killed by an otter, and had a large piece bitten out of the shoulder.

But the otter is as much a land-animal as a water-animal, and is responsible for the killing-off of much vermin, in addition to the many eels he gets in the river. So he does some good, and it would be a pity if this picturesque and interesting mammal were exterminated.

Not the least interesting of the animals the angler is familiar with is the diminutive bat, or flitter-mouse, winging its erratic flight by the river as it chases the flies in the dusk. Sometimes the bat will take an angler's fly as he throws it in the air behind him prior to casting it towards a trout. The little creatures are more numerous than the casual observer would imagine. I recall once making an all-night fishing excursion, but before midnight the sky became so overcast with heavy clouds that it was impossible to continue. So I and my companion resolved to try to sleep until dawn. We found a cave not far away, so into it we went and composed ourselves as well as we could for a short nap. It was no use. The cave seemed to be alive with thousands of bats, flittering in and out, almost brushing our cheeks now and then, and ever uttering their faint yet eerie squeak as they flew. It was all very weird, and gave us to think of vampires, and we soon got out of it. I remember after that I climbed an ancient tree, and actually dozed for an hour or two in an accommodating fork thereof, several feet above the dew-laden grass.

There is the squirrel, too, with his bright eyes and bushy tail. He may sometimes be seen in the riverside woods; but your angler will get but a mere glimpse of him. For one thing, during the fishing season the trees are usually in full leaf, and the little red-coated animal can easily hide himself in the boskage, and it is difficult to follow his movements with the eye as he jumps from branch to branch, or shins up the far side of a tree-stem.

These are the chief of the mammals the average

fisherman may encounter in the lowlands. Farther
north, in the wilder highlands, he may catch a
distant glimpse of the noble red deer, or the dainty
gentle roe; but then only a comparatively small
proportion of anglers get so far afield.

SNOWDROPS

(In Springwood Park)

But yesterday pure driven snow
  White-carpeted the glade;
Then came the south-wind's gentle blow,
A wintry sun—a scarce-felt glow—
  An early spring-day made.

Then soon the mantling snow had fled
  To swell the Teviot's flow;
And from the earth there sprang instead
White dancing stars, where once lay spread
  The still and glitt'ring snow.

I lingered, 'raptured, in the glade,
  List'ning, as in a dream;
Myriads of snowdrops, in the shade,
Seemed to be singing, as they swayed,
  In cadence with the stream:

" Emblems of purity, we bring
  Our gifts to Nature's shrine;
We come—forerunners of the spring,
Our modest flow'rets offering
  Promise of Hope divine."

AND THE FLORA:

Come with me for a stroll down the track the fishermen take to the river when on angling intent. We need not take our fishing-rods, as it is too early in the year for the trout-fisher to be looking for sport. Trout have not recovered from their lean time of winter, which means short commons for them, and they are not yet fit for either sport or the table. Give them another month or two, with sunshine, and surface-feeding on the plentiful supply of flies which they will find, and their glistening flanks will assume a glory of golden hues and pink spots. They will have grown stronger, and be more worthy to adorn the angler's creel.

The river is high, swollen by the vernal rains which took away the last of the snow from the low-lying ground; but the hollow dens and ravines of the hills are still full of snow, which will feed the river for some days to come. There will be opportunities for hooking a few spring salmon for the fortunate few, when the waters have abated somewhat.

The fisherman's track leads us down a glen. The braes on each side of us will in due time be spangled with a creamy foam of massed primroses, and a little later the pink wild rose will shed its petals so thickly that the ground will seem as though the sun's dawn-blush had stained the mossy carpet.

To-day as we approach the dense blackthorn thicket its white blossoms hang over the still leafless trees like a bridal veil, and give promise that the spring is nigh. Farther on, we pass a copse where the broom grows, and there are clumps of the prickly gorse, the flower buds on which are swollen and need only a few days of warm sun to bring out their yellow glory. Even now there is the gleam of a yellow star from the bush, to remind us that the winter is past.

On we go, into the woods that skirt the river bank. The trees are bare and leafless, save for last year's brown and withered leaves on the beeches, noble trees standing out boldly with their silver-grey trunks and far-spreading branches. The young buds will soon sprout now, and, as they unfold, their delicate shimmering greenery will displace the dead russet leaves, which even now are falling and rustling against our feet as we pass on our way. There are great sticky buds on the horse-chestnuts, and purpling buds on the elm-trees, but they are not nearly ripe for bursting. The catkins on the alders hang like golden rain, and the slender shoots of the willows are resplendent with their silvery velvet adornments—" Siller saughs wi' downy buds," as Tannahill has it in one of his songs.

The year is yet too young for wild flowers in the woods, but there are a few blooms of the coltsfoot where we crossed the road which passes the end of the wood.

But let us turn aside from the river bank and follow the narrow path which takes us deeper into the woodlands, so that we may see if the snowdrops are out. We soon come to them, and the scene makes us pause in sheer admiration of its beauty. 'Twas but yesterday and the snow was lying, like a blanket, keeping the plants warm. Now, amidst the sheltering trees, the ground is clad with snow-drops in myriads, hanging their green-tipped petals modestly, their heads and the slender spikes of green swaying gently to the zephyr. 'Tis a scene of charm, and a rich reward for our tramp by wet riverside paths and the damp tracks of the woods in the still young year.

.   .   .   .

We traverse the same road with our fishing-rod some weeks later on, and, as evidence of the fisherman's optimism, we carry a creel strapped over the shoulder.

There is a great change since we were last here. The blackthorn thicket is now dense with foliage, and under the trees there are primroses lingering, gleaming in the shade like fragments of moonlight broken from the moonbeams of yesternight. Dark-eyed dog-tooth violets are in plenty; the hawthorn is breaking into fragrant blossoming, the bees being at work amongst pink-flushed blooms. The gorse shines gold in the copse.

The woods are carpeted with wood-sorrel and anemone, their dainty little flowers showing a pattern of bright specks beneath the trees, which are now a wealth of all the hues of green—pale green, olive-green and dark green—of beech and larch, elm and chestnut, and the evergreen firs and hollies.

The ferns and the brackens are uncoiling their graceful fronds, and cowslips shake their dainty bedewed clusters of bloom in the pasture, where cuckoo-flowers vie with them in elegance and delicate beauty; and down by the waterside, where the little spring bubbles forth from the high bank, the forget-me-nots are flourishing, their masses of pale blue reminding us of the eyes of some fair daughter of our hill-country.

When we reach the river and commence our fishing we are enchanted with the wealth of flowers from the golden kingcups, opened wide to absorb the warm rays of the morning sun. And having feasted our eyes on the resplendent flora we turn to the waters, in the hope of securing a few trout.

There are days in May, when the sun is warm and the waters are fining down to summer-level, when one is tempted to sit on the river bank and to watch the stream flowing gently past, and to listen to its murmuring song. The bluebells are in full flower on the fringe of the wood where it begins to rise towards the hill, and almost as far as the eye can see their stems are bending to the breeze in waves, until one has an impression of an azure sea. The air is redolent with the heavy perfume of the flowers, intoxicating, almost inducing to drowsiness.

When flaming June comes the trees are in full leaf, and few flowers will be found beneath their dense shade; but in the open spaces the air is full of the scent of meadow-sweet, and the honeysuckle shows on the hedges and in the copses. The reeds on the marge of the river have grown man-high, and the angler has ample cover as he plies his rod during the warm evenings. The willow-herb sports its tall and gay spikes of bloom in the pebbly channel from which the shrinking river has receded, and yellow splashes of colour from the marsh-marigolds in the sluggish backwater give relief to the eye.

As autumn approaches there are very few wild flowers to be seen near the river or on the way there. The time of fruition is near at hand; the grasses and reeds are seeding; there are reddening fruits on the rowan and the wild cherry; the haws in the hedgerow are russet-hued on the side nearer the sun, and will soon be red; and the hips on the briers are also turning a ruddy hue.

Soon the woodlands will be a riot of colour, and even now one may see a few leaves of the elm assuming a saffron tint, and beech leaves becoming a russet-brown, where the chill of a slight night frost has caught them.

To the angler the autumn is the saddest time of the year, since although he may enjoy the beauties and wonders of the colouring nature gives to the landscape, yet he knows that soon he must put away his rod until another season comes round. But he has his memories of joyous times in the spring and summer that have passed, when his reel sang its merry tune, and he oft returned home with the spoils of a happy day of sport spent close to nature's heart, when the wild birds and beasts he met, and the sweet flowers he saw, helped to make of his angling day something more than the mere pursuit of his finny quarry.

AT THE GATEHEUGH

THE GATEHEUGH, FROM BEMERSYDE, WITH THE EILDON HILLS

[*page* 150

THE BIRTH OF THE PRIMROSE

Soft moonbeams gently wooed the dews of night,
Where, shyly trembling, glinting all a-shake,
They coyly hid from Luna's amorous light,
In a deep glen, beneath the thorny brake.

When April skies were bright, one joyous morn,
I peeped into the greening hawthorn brake,
And there looked up, dew-lipped, just newly born,
Pale primrose stars, their eyes but half awake.

Sweet modest childings of moondust and dew,
That shyly hide your heads from noonday's glare,
Your pale dewed petals glow with love that grew
When moonbeams kissed the dewdrops light as air.

CHAPTER X

AT THE GATEHEUGH

COME with me to the Gateheugh, and you shall see the bonniest bit of trouting water in the whole course of Tweed's hundred miles or so of sylvan and pastoral beauty, a stretch of water which is not only good to look upon, and a delight for its scenic glories, but where you will find trout of size, lusty and strong, and the most gallant fighters in the river.

From above the Gledswood Boat Pool the river begins a mighty sweep round the site of old Melrose Abbey. Not the venerable ruin, now the tourist-haunted Mecca of the American globe-trotter, who spends a few moments there with Baedeker in hand and deems he has seen all, and understands all that the relic means, but the abbey of an earlier date, of which no outward vestige remains.

The river here makes almost a circle in its course, and, in doing so, its outside curve impinges force-fully upon and erodes the hill of Bemersyde, crowned by the ancient Border keep so late the home of the great soldier who now rests in quiet, peaceful Dryburgh, not so far away, alongside that other indomitable Scot, who wielded a weapon even more powerful and mightier than the sword of the warrior.

You cannot see it from here, down by the

waterside, but if you make a detour, and put a stout heart to a " stey brae," you will come to the little gate on the hill-road from whence Sir Walter was wont to view the vale of Tweed, looking over the ribbon-like stream in the depths below, and the panorama beyond Melrose and the triple crowns of Eildon, to the dim and distant purpling hills—as fair a scene at daybreak or upon a summer's eve as eye e'er gazed upon. 'Tis related that when the remains of the great writer were being conveyed to their last resting-place by this road the horses stopped, of their own accord, as if they sensed that the spirit of their departed master would wish to pause and contemplate the view once more, ere he passed on to the end of his last journey.

We started, however, at the Gledswood Boat Pool, and must climb the hill some other day, when trout are not in season, and trout-fishing does not call us to postpone all other outlets for our energy.

We are on the right bank of the river, with Old Melrose and its woodlands behind us, resplendent in their summer boskage, hiding fox and pheasant —unhappy combination perhaps—and many a rare feathered visitant. Here you may hear the woodpecker tapping the tree-stems, and the cuckoo's not unpleasing note in spring, and many a cheerful warbler who makes the air ring with his carolling. Adjoining the wood is a wide " haugh," formed by the alluvial deposits of ages, its green springy turf providing an acceptable open space between the wood and the towering scaur facing us on the far bank of the river.

'Tis said that in the days of eld, when the country-side was wilder and less cultivated than now, the kite—or "gled," to give it its local name—had its eyrie on the scaur-face, and gave its name to the neighbouring lands of Gledswood. It is believable, for even in recent years we have known hawks to nest there, in an almost unapproachable spot, tempting adventurous youths to scale the perilous heights, at risk of life or limb, in hope of securing forbidden trophies.

Well did the monks of old choose the sites whereon they dwelt. They were among the pleasantest places in this isle of ours, retired from the turmoil of the world as they knew it, and quiet retreats even now, amidst amenities which might remind us of the Garden of Eden. Plenitude of wood for shelter and for winter fires and comfort and the roasting of the beeves, crystal streams which never failed to provide water to drive the miller's wheel and—what was of much importance on days of fasting from flesh-meats—an abundance of fresh-water fish for the refectory, trout of the finest for size and flavour, and salmon most of the year round. Doubtless the rich soil of the low-lying lands gave them all the tillage they needed, and pasture for the kine, while the lordly stag and the roe abounded, and the larder never lacked a good fat haunch of venison.

Enough of these digressions, and let us to the river, which from the Boat Pool runs deep and placid for some distance, providing a fine piece of water for a salmon, and, in the spring, excellent trouting water. Then begin the streams of the Gateheugh proper—wild, rough water, pouring through narrow channels, tearing over rocks and boulders, and interspersed with pot-holes where great trout lie in summer-time, and eddies where you are sure to hook fish when you can reach them. But have a care when fishing here. You are on treacherous ground, and your zeal and keenness may lead you on too far, to find that the weight of rushing water over the slippery stones is more than the strength of your muscles will bear, and you lose your foothold, to your undoing.

We have recollections of one such occasion when an incautious step resulted in a ducking. It was a bright hot day, and the angler was hardy enough —after stripping in the wood and wringing out as much water from his clothing as he possibly could —to go on fishing, fortunately with no untoward results.

The Gateheugh is practically unfishable until the water is at low summer-level. There was one spot, which we knew as " The Dish," that would always give us an indication whether it was worth our while to fish there. " The Dish " was well named —a nice little pool between two wild deep-running streams which converged towards a large rock, over which streams and pool met and poured their waters into a sort of deep gully. If the top of the rock was exposed a few inches one could always count on getting a good trout or two, either just at the lip of " The Dish," or on the far side of the turgid stream below it, although to land them was always a matter of anxiety, requiring skill and the exercise of delicate handling of the rod to bring the fish through the heavy waters with success.

We have fished the Gateheugh in bright sunshine with the worm. We have fished it, too, with the " creeper "—that fearsome and unlovely lure which is often so deadly for a brief season in May or early June. We have taken noble trout with these lures. We have at times used a small artificial minnow in a very bright water under a glaring sun, and met with some success, but this mode of fishing has always been resorted to as a last hope, when fly-fishing has been impossible, and the "creeper" season spent. Grand trout of $1\frac{1}{2}$ lb. and $1\frac{1}{4}$ lb. and many a pounder have we encreeled here with these lures, and many more have we lost which—to quote a phrase I have heard used by a well-known Tweedside fisher and angling writer whom I often met on the river—were "nearer a pound-and-a-half than a pound"! These were always the lost ones.

Yet our catches were insignificant to what old Tom Stoddart was wont to take when he visited the Gateheugh, of which he had a very high opinion, and with good reason.

Stoddart has written that on one occasion— 4th June 1855, to be precise—he caught eighteen trout weighing 19 lb., with the worm, in three hours. The "toppers" of this basket were nine fish which drew the scale at $14\frac{1}{2}$ lb., or over $1\frac{1}{2}$ lb. of an average. Fishing a month later, also with worm, he had thirty-four trout which aggregated 25 lb. Trout must have been more numerous then —it is over seventy years ago—and it must not be forgotten that Stoddart could charm fish from the water with rod and line.

You will get no baskets of 25 lb. nowadays, be you ever so skilled a fisherman, albeit the Gateheugh is not yet—nor ever will be so long as Tweed runs clear—without trout in plenty in its pools and streams.

If you would enjoy the Gateheugh at its best you must go some quiet summer eve with your rod, and fish with fly only to tempt the trout. You may, if you wish, essay the dry-fly style, and " fish the rise "; but you will find it no easy task to float your fly, owing to the inevitable " drag " of your line in this tangle of rushing streams and eddies. Perhaps you were better to fish after the wet-fly fashion after all—and I am sometimes inclined to the opinion that it requires more river-craft to fish properly by this method than it does to fish the dry-fly way. At any rate, to fish the wet-fly way with the greatest success the angler must be well learned in the habits of trout, and he must have good knowledge of where they lie in different heights of the water, so that he can go after them confidently and seek them in their lairs. So shall the creel be filled.

Where no trout are rising you may get them to rise to a dry fly—I see the purist holding up his hands in horror at the heresy—but in water such as this your line may be swirled out of the reach of the fish before he has time to dart from his hide and seize your fly, or the drag may give him timely warning that things are not what they seem. Hence my opinion that to sink your flies in the right places in such streams as these may show you a heavier creel at the end of your summer evening's sport; and I speak from experience.

There comes back to me a vivid memory of one notable summer's eve on the Gateheugh. The sun was going down, and the slanting shadows of the woods were almost on the river's fringe, although there was time and to spare before the sun went down behind the Eildon Hills.

It was a peaceful evening, with a clear atmosphere and an unclouded sky. Red Spinners were dancing, myriads of them, in the rays of light, joyous in their all-too-brief spell of life. The songbirds were warbling with that mellow tone so often noticeable on a warm June night—when foliage is full, and there is cool shelter in the shade of the branches, and naught to disturb them—as if they were glad to be alive, satisfied with all things, full-fed and happy.

When I reached the Gateheugh streams the pleasing song of the reel greeted me, and I observed that my old friend " The Lurcher " was there, busy playing a trout he had hooked in " The Dish." The Dominie, too, had been tempted out to try his fortune. One rarely saw his rubicund figure on the water those days, for he was not so active as he once was, and wading had begun to have terrors for him. But there he was, whipping away not unskilfully, and evidently in full enjoyment of his sport, for he had always had a keen zest for it.

The presence of these brothers of the craft did not disconcert me, for there was plenty of room for all, and they would not unduly disturb the water for anyone following up behind. So I leisurely strolled to the very top of the Gateheugh, fitted up my rod, and selected what I deemed to be a suitable cast.

Against all the canons of the quidnuncs we were fishing across and down the stream, for to fish the Gateheugh upstream fashion on a warm evening, wading against heavy-flowing waters, is making a labour of a recreation; and, after all, we used to find that we lost fewer trout by fishing " fine and far," across and down the river, than by fishing up with a necessarily shorter line.

Here, where I begin, is the end of a long stretch of flat water, which suddenly breaks up on a rocky bottom, spreading out into a congeries of pot-holes, little runlets and eddies. In a low water, by careful wading, you can manage to reach the Bemersyde bank, and, as you cross, throwing your fly here and there, you may pick up a trout or two. There are dangers when fishing here in the gloaming. The fascination of the place seems to hold you, and you go on and on, from rock to rock, and tiny pool to tiny pool, led on by seeing a trout rising and raising a filmy spray now and again. You may get him or miss him, but there is ever another to try for. You forget yourself, maybe, in your concentration on the trout, until you find it is almost dark and you cannot pick your way back.

It is not by any means a pleasing situation to be in, to find yourself standing on a projecting rock, with swirling waters all around you, when you cannot see either bank of the river in the gathering mirk of the brief northern summer night. You have a fair idea of where you are, and you let down a leg on this side of your rock and then the other, to find that each time you are going too deep, and the prospect of dropping down into a deep hole, with waders filling to weight you down, is not alluring. I remember being marooned in this fashion for what seemed hours one June night. Probably it was not more than half-an-hour really, but it was even then too long to be pleasant. Fortunately for me, Thomson, the keeper, knew I was on the water, and had come down to look for me.

He must have been lynx-eyed to have seen me in the semi-darkness, or he may have heard me splashing around. So he called out an inquiry as to who was there, and I told him my plight. He guided me out by the simple expedient of walking back up the river and calling me at frequent intervals to make a line to the spot whence his voice seemed to come—I could not see him; and so I safely reached the shore. It was an experience, and a lesson.

But it is light enough as we commence our fishing this pleasant summer eve, and with a Corncrake fly as leader on the cast, a Woodcock and Harelug, and a Blae Wing with yellow body as droppers, I wade in and essay a few short casts.

It is soon enough yet, but I see a trout rising far out, and this gives me hope of early sport, so I work steadily across, being rewarded with a half-pounder on the Woodcock, with a long line out over a stream on which the sun is shining brightly. After capturing another trout of about the same size, I waded back to the bank, for the purpose of fishing downstream from my first starting-point.

Nothing of any moment occurred, and I saw very few trout move until I came to " The Dish." There my hopes ran high, but there was no sign of a rising fish, and had I been fishing with a dry fly I should doubtless have passed on. But I knew my water, and so, carefully throwing right over to the far side of the pool, I allowed my flies to sink, and the current straightened out the line, bringing my flies round to the " hing," or lip of " The Dish," where I felt sure there would be a goodly trout on the look-out.

Oh, oh! There he goes, and a right good one too, well hooked. Over the lip of " The Dish " into the turmoil of the deep rapid stream below, jerking off yards of line from the reel in his frantic endeavours to break away. I give him plenty of law, holding the rod-point well up, and he leaves the stream and dashes over the river, leaping dangerously near some jagged rocks in his efforts to free himself of the barb. Down goes my rod-top and he is thwarted, and at last he is under control and being led back through the stream. Be careful here, for he makes another flurry; but if the heavy water has its advantages on the side of the trout, in sometimes enabling him to regain his freedom, on the other hand, if the hook holds, he is more quickly tired out, battling against the strong current. At last he is beaten and led through the shallows and up the narrow shingly strand. He is a beauty of 1½ lb., plump and gloriously golden, hooked on the Blae Wing.

"The Dish" has been little disturbed in the playing of this trout, for he went over into the stream below immediately he was hooked, so back we go to that favourite hold, and within a few minutes raise another, whose tactics are similar to those of the one just previously landed. The Corncrake is the successful fly this time, and the fish is soon ashore, proving to be a nice one of 1¼ lb., not quite so plump as the other, being a little leaner in the flank maybe, but a desirable capture withal. A merry spin he had given, and the angler's hopes were rising.

Another cast or two in " The Dish " before passing on, without a further rise; so I tried a little lower down, in what we knew as the " Tree Cast," there being a solitary and lonely plane-tree on the bank just behind.

Fortune was kind. In a very short time I had creeled five more trout, ranging from 1 lb. to $\frac{1}{2}$ lb., all on the Woodcock fly, every trout a game fighter in splendid condition.

The late-evening rise had not yet taken place, but with a basket of about 8 lb. of excellent trout I was content, and began to think of plodding my way homeward.

Passing down the river I overtook " The Lurcher," and although I had been luckier than he had, for once, with the bigger fish, he had done well and had secured an excellent lot of trout. He was surprised that I was leaving off before the late rise was due, and expressed his intention of retracing his footsteps to the " flat " water of the Boat Pool, where, when the night-moths and sedge-flies begin to move, there is always a certainty of a few trout on an evening in May or June, and some good ones too. So I wished him luck and left him.

I was satisfied, however, with what I had taken. They were sufficient for my needs, they had given me a delightful evening's sport, and what more could reasonable angler want?

However, as I wended my way downstream, I was tempted to try another cast, as I thought I had seen a big trout rise far out on the flat water above the Monks' Ford. To reach it required wading and a long line, and I was not successful in hooking him.

I was wading back to shore when I noticed something unusual on the river-bed, which was composed of bright clean gravel at that point, and the water being crystal clear I could see every stone.   Investigation revealed two large lampreys, holding on to a large stone with their sucker-like mouths, and although I endeavoured to move them, with my landing-net, I could not do so. They were too large to scoop out with my trout-net, anyway, even had I been able to induce them to release their hold of the stone.

Lampreys are not rare visitants to the river, which they ascend for spawning purposes in early summer, but they were the first I had ever seen so far up the water.

But here I take down my rod, or I shall be tempted to remain for the late evening rise, and, maybe, to fish on through the later hours and perhaps to midnight or beyond, this pleasant summer eve. And so home, by way of the glen with its wimpling burn, and the winding woodland path, where the scent of wild rose and sweetbrier suffuses the air, and the night-owl is already calling in the tree-tops. The season is yet young, and there will be other nights on which to ply the rod.

UP IN THE MORNING
EARLY

A SUMMER DAWN ON TWEED

Like as a veil o'er blushing bride
    Diaphanous mists, faint rosy-hued,
Coyly enwrap the river's tide
    With mystery deep imbued.

The dawn comes up o'er Bemersyde,
    Enriched with gold, heralding day;
And ardent Phœbus, in his pride,
    Soon rends the veil away.

As Tweed's fair glory shows revealed,
    The song-birds blithe their chorus sing;
And in the woodland depths, concealed,
    Make bridal carolling.

The angler, patient for the dawn,
    Now woos his sport with gentle skill;
And, from the gleaming river drawn,
    Creels trout gleam brighter still.

Yet Nature o'er him weaves her spell,
    Arresting play of rod and line—
Revealing, where his rapt eyes dwell,
    The works of the Divine.

CHAPTER XI

UP IN THE MORNING EARLY

WHY trout should be eager to take small red worms in the dawn of midsummer days, when the water is very low and brilliantly clear, was always a mystery to me. I used to wonder how the worms got into the river, and came to the conclusion —whether rightly or wrongly I do not know—that the worm is enticed from its hole in the earth by the tempting moisture on the dew-laden grass, and the venturesome crawler goes exploring in the cool damp. Sometimes it goes too far, and falls over the brink into the stream, to its own undoing, and the delectation of a roaming trout.

Charles Kingsley has written that, wandering from home, against parental advice, a

"... feckless hairy oubit cam' hirpling by the linn,
A swirl o' wind cam' doun the glen, and blew that oubit in."

The small red worm that strays too far from home appears to meet with a like fate.

However the worms get there, it is a certainty that they are present, and trout are on the look-out for them with the first grey awakening of the dawn, as is amply evidenced by the success many anglers meet with in the earliest hours of the day, fishing with the worm.

I write here of worm-fishing in midsummer, and

in clear water. The midsummer nights across the Scottish Border are very brief, and you may find it quite light at two of the clock on a June or July morning, if the sky be unclouded.

Many times when returning from an evening's fly-fishing, which has extended until midnight, have I met the worm-fisher on his way to the river, and the angler who desires to creel a few trout with the aid of the worm must therefore be up in the morning early, and be ready to start his pursuit of the trout not much later than one of the clock. Fine tackle is required, and the fishing must be done cautiously and carefully upstream.

If no other angler has stolen a march on you and passed up the water before you, and you wade quietly up, through the shallows, you may often see many large trout in the fringes of the streams, where there is scarcely enough water flowing to cover their dorsal fins. You may sometimes come quite close to them before they sense your presence, either by their acute sight or the vibrations of earth or water caused by your footfall. Then they will scurry off into the deep water, making such a wave as they go that you know they are bigger trout than you have had the luck to catch for many a day.

The description of trout-fishing with the worm in the early morn of which I speak here must not be confused with that practised more or less the season round in burns and small waters. In the Tweed it is mostly confined to the period commencing at the latter end of May, and on through June and July, when the weather is fine and the water low.

During this time, if the weather be congenial and of a moderately high temperature, you may get good trout as soon as the day dawns, and may continue with some degree of success until the sun is high.

The great thing to remember is that there is little prospect of success if you keep to the main channel of the river, since the trout, in the early hours, when the river is low or attenuated by drought, will be found lying in shallow ripples and detached runlets where, at a first glance, you would not think there would be enough water to cover their backs or hide them.

Hence considerable craft and skill are required for success, and the angler must of necessity keep as well hidden from them as he can, and must almost literally creep up behind them as he casts his bait, since trout at this period are in prime condition, plump and well-fed, and consequently at their wariest.

My old fishing acquaintance, who was known to all our village as " The Mavis," was a very skilled angler with the worm in clear water, and often in the summer months I had heard his iron-shod brogues clattering down the village street towards the river, some time after midnight. Very often, at that time, I was preparing for bed, after I had been out on the river fishing with the fly until nigh twelve o'clock.

While I always preferred fly-fishing to any other means of angling for trout, there were often times when, after a long drought, fly-fishing even at night would not allure the fish, and, if a basket were to be obtained at all, there was no option but to employ the worm as the most likely means of plenishing the creel.

So, being in such a predicament, I arranged with " The Mavis " that we should go out one morning together, and that he should give me an exhibition of the methods whereby he gained success when others failed. Not that I was ignorant of the process entirely, for I had prosecuted most methods of fishing for trout at their proper times and seasons; but I deemed that a few hours out with the old fellow would be interesting, and at the same time instructive.

Therefore, off we went one morning before the dawn, accoutred with waders and brogues, with our rods already put together, and casting lines in order. We had a wood to traverse on our way to the water, but if a fishing-rod is carried butt-end first, with anything like reasonable care, there is not much risk of breaking the top-piece even in the dark.

We had about a mile to walk before we reached our starting-point, and by the time we wetted our lines there was just a faint greyness in the eastern sky, heralding the break of day. In the wood there was now and again the chirp of a bird to be heard, a sure sign that the dawn was nigh. Very soon the whole world would resound with the songs of thrush and blackbird, linnet and bullfinch, wren and robin, and many another.

" I'll try her in yon ripple just abune the ford," said " The Mavis," " an' then wade up the middle and fish the shallows towards the bank. Keep well ahint me, an' oot o' sicht as weel as ye can," he exhorted, as he slipped into the water knee-high.

He was interesting to watch. His rod was a two-handed one, which, although light in build, was of a stiff nature. His casting line was of the finest, and his hooks were of the well-known Stewart pattern—three small hooks—on which he had deftly impaled a bright red and well-scoured worm.

With very little more line out than the length of his rod, he heaved the bait forward rather than cast it, allowing it to drop into the water as gently almost as a snowflake—the bait was not weighted —and gradually raised the point of his rod as the worm floated downstream towards him with the current. I should mention that he had tied a small piece of white calico to his line, where the gut was attached, as an indicator—the light being poor— to show how his bait was running.

Where he was fishing the stream glided over a gravelly shallow, not more than six inches deep. Suddenly he was all alert: his little white flag was at a standstill. He paused for the merest fraction of a second before giving the rod the slightest twitch with his wrist, and a splashing and spluttering told of a trout hooked. It was very soon in the net, and weighed half-a-pound or so.

As soon as the trout was hooked, " The Mavis " had led it down the water for a few yards, skilfully avoiding any disturbance of the stream above. Then, after creeling the fish, he put a fresh worm on his hooks, made a few steps forward, and the process was repeated, another half-pounder meeting with the fate of its fellow. Not a bad beginning.

Then a little farther up we went, to where a long deep pool split up into rippling shallow breaks streaming towards the opposite bank of the river. This was a more difficult place to fish, as it required a longish line to reach the edges of the streams, and there was the additional disadvantage that the angler could not get behind the trout. But the sun was not up, and the light was but dim yet, throwing no shadows, so the angler drew a little more line from his reel, gave his bait a good swing forward, letting some of the slack line he held in his hand run out as the bait touched the water and was held by the current. His tell-tale flag stopped almost immediately; there was a brief flurry, and in a very short time another trout—this time one of three-quarters of a pound—was added to the creel.

Although he tried these shallows carefully again, no more fish came to his lures, and he suggested that we might try the water a few hundred yards higher up. So we scrambled along the rocky marge of the river, passing deep pools which were useless for our purpose, although generally productive at night with the fly.

"Aye, man! I've seen some grand troots gotten wi' the flee just by yon swirl ower the rock opposite tae us. It's a grand cast in the spring, when there is a full river; an' whiles I hae killed ten pounds or sae when the rise was on, an' every yin o' them as big as a mackerel. But it's nae use tryin' tae fish it wi' the worm. We'll hae a cast beyond the bend, just ayont the Haliwiel Throat."

So on we went, past the bend, and I looked for something interesting to happen here. The river at this point makes a sharp double turn, and, in doing so, becomes confined for a short distance in a narrow gorge which at night is rather awesome, and perhaps best avoided. The water is deep and turbulent, and pours into a very deep pool where salmon lurk the year round, and where very heavy trout swim, but are seldom caught, except with worm in a flood-water.

Just above the narrow gorge there are several little shallow runs, overflows from the main stream which throws itself with some force and violence against the opposite bank, and here " The Mavis " thought there might be a chance of a trout or two.

He was right. He had stepped down into the deeper water as far as it was safe to go. He then waded up a few yards, casting his bait gently, as he went, into the ripples on the fringes of the stream. I saw him heave the bait forward into a very thin run—a mere trickle—just a few feet above a tumbling, swirling eddy. There was a sudden gleam of silvery light from the sides of a great trout, and in less time than I can write of it " The Mavis" was out of the river and on to the bank, following his fish in careful haste down the heavy rushing stream to which it had dashed, while his reel was in truth ringing out merry music.

It was a lesson in the playing of a big fish on fine tackle to watch him, as he let it expend its energy for a while in the heavy water. Then he manœuvred it into the quieter waters of the deep pool below, where the turmoil of the stream above induced a back-water, into which he led the fish, and eventually safely netted it.

It was a magnificent trout of 2 lb. 10 oz., and its captor, although saying little about it, was mightily pleased, as he was certainly entitled to be.

The excitement of playing and landing such a notable fish seemed to have taken some of the life out of " The Mavis," who was no longer a young man, and he sat down on the trunk of a fallen tree, while he leisurely filled a pipe and lit it. When he had got it going to his satisfaction he could not refrain from lifting the trout out of the creel, and again admiring its glorious proportions. It was a real beauty and in prime summer condition.

After a brief rest we resumed our pursuit of sport, and fished some broken water which yielded several small trout; but these "The Mavis" handled roughly, I thought, and apparently with contempt, as he hauled them ashore.

The big trout had unsettled him, it seemed to me, and as the sun was now well up in the sky I suggested we had seen the best of the sport, and might as well make tracks for home and an early breakfast. We—or I should rather say "The Mavis"—had been fishing for a little more than three hours, actually, and had about six pounds of trout in the creel, thanks in large part to the big fish. This, however, was not a bad catch for the time of the year, and the short time we had been out.

So we wended our way home, by way of the wood and across the pastures beyond. In the woods the birds had long since ceased their morning chorus, and were busy fetching and carrying, for the most part, for the many hungry young mouths gaping for food in tree and bush. At the back of the wood, as we climbed the fence, scores of rabbits scudded off from their feeding-grounds as they caught sight of us, and a couple of pheasants rocketted up into a tree with a note of warning. A bright-eyed red squirrel scrambled up the trunk of a Scots fir, and chattered angrily at us as it sat in safety on a branch well out of reach.

UP IN THE MORNING EARLY

As we plodded over the dew-sodden pasture we came across the first mushrooms of the season, forced into growth doubtless by the intense heat of recent days, and warm humid nights, and a goodly helping of the dainty fungus soon topped the fish in the creel.

Trout fresh caught, and mushrooms newly gathered from 'midst the morning dews, for breakfast —surely something worth being up in the morning early for !

TALES FROM TWEEDSIDE

A MUCKLE FUSH

Young Tammas was a fisher stout
    Who dwelt by fair Tweedside;
His creel he often filled wi' trout,
For Tammas knew his way about,
    And where the big trout hide.

Now Tammas he ambitious was
    A " muckle fush " to kill.
Great trout he'd taken oft, whereas
A salmon never yet, alas !
    Had tried his angling skill.

Oft had he lingered on the brig,
    And pondered deeply why,
Although he'd captured trout and snig,
He'd ne'er had luck to catch a big
    Fine salmon wi' his fly.

He stood one autumn day and gazed
    Into a salmon pool;
And as he stood he stared, amazed,
His bulging eyes seemed almost glazed,
    For there, leading the " school,"

The biggest " fush " that e'er he saw—
    Its back as broad's a sow—
Playfully swimming, king of a'
The salmon that, so gay and braw,
    With fin Tweed's waters plough.

Though Tammas had nor rod nor line,
 In's pooch he kept a " cleek,"
With which he whiles had made design
To snatch a fush he might consign
 To pickle in peat reek.

So, boldly daring, Tammas made
 His cleek fast to a thong;
Then, wary, did the river wade,
To where the fush unheeding played
 Amongst the finny throng.

With eager glee he flung his cleek
 Into the salmon's side—
The salmon, strong and broad and sleek,
Resented Tammas's cool cheek—
 Forbye, it hurt its pride.

So, swiftly turning in its track
 That fush lashed out at Tam;
Its tail caught him a mighty smack
That knocked him over on his back
 Then gaily off it swam.

. . . . .

When Tam has had a dram or two
 He oft relates the tale,
About that fush " as broad's a soo "
That took his cleek, and felled him too—
 " 'Twas maist as big's a whale! "

But Tammas never poaches now
 When great fush are about;
He fears to meet one " broad as a sow,"
That slapped his face, and ducked him too,
 So now he sticks to trout !

ROB O' THE TROWS

|page 182

CHAPTER XII

TALES FROM TWEEDSIDE

UNDER THE BEECH TREES

IT was a night in July. There were many of the local devotees of the rod on the water, as the day had been fine and warm, yet on the humid and heavy side, and it was not surprising therefore that the evening rise had been unproductive and disappointing.

To damp all hopes of our obtaining decent creels of trout, moreover, a white mist began to curl on the pools, and there was every indication that it would become denser as the night wore on, making it impossible for further fishing that night. With the appearance of the mist the air had become somewhat chilly, and it was curious to note how first one angler, then another, drifted towards the old and wide-spreading beech-trees near the ford, where there was a sheltered sandy bank, and where, already, auld Wullie Veitch was piling up twigs he had gathered in the wood near by, preparatory to lighting a fire.

It was quite an institution, this camp-fire, on a summer night when sport was indifferent, and a strangely mixed group often gathered there, to sit on the dry sandy turf or stand around the fire gratefully absorbing the heat, smoking their pipes, and swapping stories relating to the one interest they had in common. I sometimes joined them, and picked up many a wrinkle which was to prove useful in my fishing.

There had been a spell of silence while some of the usually loquacious ones were filling up and lighting their pipes prior to settling down; and it was the Dominie's voice which first broke the spell.

" It is a queer thing, what a haud this fishing will gain over a man," he remarked, quite *apropos* of nothing.

" Ye will all mind Jock the tailor, who, although born within an arrow-shot of Tweed, only took to trout-fishing long after he was married and had a family growing up; but when he had once begun to experience the pleasures known only to fishermen he got so keen and enthusiastic that nothing could keep him away from the water when trout were rising, and he did his best to make up for his wasted youth—wasted as far as fishing goes, I should say."

" Aye, and I mind when he wad stand on the brig and jeer at us, and ca' us puir silly fools, wasting our time thrashing the watter and, as he thought, ne'er catchin' fish," chimed in " The Mavis."

Not heeding the interruption, the Dominie proceeded:

" The Shirra's daughter had ordered a new riding-habit from him. And, mind you, Jock was a skilly man at his trade, and made for many of the nobility and gentry in the county. In due time the lady called at Jock's shop to be fitted. This process had been gone through twice, and arrangements were being made for a third and final fitting, and the question came up as to what day and time would be most convenient, to which the obliging Jock replied that any day would suit him, so long as she did not call between the hours of eleven A.M. and two P.M.

"'But why,' asked the lady—'why not during those hours?'

"'Well, ma'am,' chuckled the wielder of the goose-iron, 'ye see that's the time o' day when the troots are risin' the noo.'"

"Man, that was awfu' like Jock," said "The Lurcher," who as a rule never had much to say.

And then, in his shy and diffident way, "The Lurcher" asked if we had heard that one about the fellow doon by Cheviotfoot, and what happened to his "take," which he thought was sure to win a prize at the local competition.

It usually took "The Lurcher" a long time to tell his rare stories, and I will not endeavour to reproduce his tale as he told it. For one thing, his language was very archaic, and might not, in these days of the Oxford accent and wirelessed English, be understood by many.

But this is the gist of it.

In the village mentioned by "The Lurcher" practically every man and boy is a fisherman, which is not to be wondered at with so many delightful small streams and hill burns, flowing down from the Cheviots, within reach. There is great rivalry amongst the anglers, and every year the peak of interest in the fishing culminates in a great fishing competition.

After a long day's fishing one of the experts amongst them, who had been among the hill burns, turned his steps homeward, confident that his creel would make a good showing at the weighing-in which was to take place in the village hall.

He had time to spare, so he bethought him to hie to his cottage first, to remove some of the dirt, and to tidy himself up generally after his long scramble. Anyway, he would be all the better for a wash and brush-up, as he was pretty sure he would have to go forward before the assembly to receive a prize.

Arrived at his home, he put his creel and fishing-gear aside, and went " ben the hoose," where he could be heard splashing and blowing contentedly in the caller water.

Soon he was ready to shoulder his creel again ere departing for the " weigh-in," but, as he took hold of the shoulder-strap, he lifted the lid of the creel to have one more peep at the speckled beauties which he was confident were to win him a trophy. He was amazed to find his creel was empty!

With a roar he cried out to the guidwife, asking in not very gentle tones what had become of his troots.

" Sure," replied the dame, " I've juist taen off their heids and cleaned and gutted them ready for the frying-pan, juist as I aye dae, Sandy, my man, when ye bring hame a dish o' troots."

Sandy did not win a prize that time, but the trout looked very good and tempting as he sat down to supper with the guidwife that night. The story of how Sandy was cheated of his reward for a good basket, however, soon got abroad, and it will be a long time before he hears the last of it.

When " The Lurcher " had finished his story he gathered up his rod and landing-net, expressing his opinion that he didna think it was any use stopping there, as there would be no more trout rising that night, and like as not the " rook," or mist, would be thick on the water at day-dawn, and therefore the fishing would be useless. So he went off home and to his bed, like a wise man.

After the departure of " The Lurcher," up spoke " The Mavis," who, at any rate, was never backward or self-conscious.

" D'ye ken," he began, " what happened betwixt oor freend Wullie wha has juist gane, and Jamie Kerr, the ither nicht?

" Weel, as ye a' ken, the twa o' them are guid at the fishin', keen as can be, an' many a guid creelful dae they take.

" But, man alive, they are that jealous o' each ither, an' the yin canna thole the ither gettin' a better take than hissel'.

" Aboot a week syne, the two o' them were fishin' late at nicht aboon the ford, and Wullie's reel was tellin' its tale of troot aifter troot bein' run an' creeled.

" This made Jamie uneasy, as he wasna gettin' any ava, sae he cried oot tae Wull:

" ' Whatna flee are ye gettin' them on, Wull? '

" And back cam Wull's answer:

" ' I dinna ken, Jamie. It's owre dark tae see! '

" Aifter a whilie Wullie's guid luck stoppit, and it was Jamie's turn tae be killin' troot aifter troot, sae Wull cried oot to Jamie, speiring whatna' flee was takin' the noo.

" But Jamie, wad ye believe it, wasna giving information away, sae he roared doon the water:

" ' The *end* flee, man; juist the *end* flee! ' "

It was the same Jamie Kerr who was the doubtful hero of a bold and daring episode.

There had been a flood a few days before, and a

few salmon had run up the river, the water being in excellent condition for fly-fishing, either for salmon or trout.

At times like this many who were seldom seen on the water when prospects were not so propitious turned out with their rods, and one of these was an ancient fisherman, rather noted, I regret to record, for his greed. But he had been, in his time, and still was, an expert with the rod.

Old Dickson had no right to fish for salmon, but he would invariably appear with a sixteen- or even eighteen-foot rod, and was not above using a salmon-fly as a lure if he deemed the coast was clear of water-bailiffs.

On the occasion of which I write, Dickson hooked and landed a nice, newly-run salmon of a little under 20 lb. weight. He looked carefully around to see if he might with safety kill the fish, and then he deliberately cut the hook from the salmon's mouth with a formidable-looking pocket-knife, and in doing so he made a wretched gash in its palate, causing it to bleed profusely.

The fish was, of course, dying, and the old man placed it in a quiet backwater, to await a chance to smuggle it home. The old rascal then changed his cast, putting on one or two trout-flies, and went on fishing for trout as though nothing had happened, and all he desired was to kill a few trout.

At this juncture Jamie Kerr came swinging along down the waterside. He stopped to make a few remarks about the sport, and spoke to the ancient fisherman. All at once he espied the salmon lying on its side in the backwater. He made a sudden dash for it, lifted it out by the gills, and crammed it into his creel, which was an unusually capacious one, and perhaps meant for such a chance as this. He then cut up through the wood, and made a bee-line for home, leaving the ancient poaching fisherman speechless and gasping with amazement.

The local men who saw the deed thought it was a good joke, and they had no sympathy for old Dickson.

Wullie Veitch had been putting more wood on the camp-fire, and looked as though he meant to settle down for the night, and as he did so he began to chuckle quietly to himself.

So " The Mavis " asked him what was ticklin' him.

" Weel," said Wullie, " I was in Purdie's tackle-shop the day, seeing aboot a repair tae ma reel, and there was two or three ithers there, haein' a crack about things in general, when the door opens, and in rushes Tam Laing, frae doon by, a' in a great hurry, and breathless like. ' Hi,' says he. ' Gie me twa o' your Mairch Broons tied on gut. *I'm wantin' tae catch a bus.*'

" He was a bit put oot at the laugh that went roond the shop, and one o' the customers remarked that Tam maun hae muckle faith in Purdie's Mairch Broons, but he dooted whether they would be much use in hauding yin o' thae new-fangled motor-sharrybangs which were noo sae common on the roads."

Wullie had another little tale he wanted us to hear.

" Purdie was tellin' us a story," he said, " aboot an auld greybeard wha used tae sit ootside a Border inn doon Kelsae way. The auld fellow aye carried a fishing-rod, seemingly takin' nae notice of what was gaun on roond aboot him, but verra intent on his business of fishin' in the rain-water barrel.

"One o' these swell Englishmen was passing at the time—fully rigged out wi' waders, brogues, muckle creel, landing-net an' a'—an' when he sees the auld man at the barrel he stops an' gazes at him wi' compassion. So he took the auld chap into the 'pub' and gied him a nip.

" 'Tell me,' said the Sassenach, in a coaxing and sympathetic way, 'do you catch many?'

" 'Ye are the seeventh the day,' was the reply."

"The Mavis" here casually remarked that she wasna gaun to be muckle use for fushin' any mair the nicht.

There was silence for a while after this, and it seemed as though the mist on the river was damping the enthusiasm, but the Dominie could always find a story or anecdote to relate suitable for the occasion.

"It is a noteworthy thing," said the Dominie, "that native Tweed anglers always refer to Tweed as if she were a woman, and it puzzles strangers to hear the local men aver, when discussing the state of the water, that she will be waxing or swelling, or that she is waning—that is to say, the river is rising or falling, as the case may be.

"In this connection a story is often told by old fishermen of the days when leistering, or 'burning the water,' as they called it, was often indulged in, and when not only professional fishermen but the lairds themselves were eager to take part in a night's leistering.

"On one occasion, as the outlook was promising,

arrangements were completed for ' burning ' the Floors water.

" The Duke was aware that his head fisherman's mother was very ill, and, being a considerate and kind employer, he told the man he need not be present unless he particularly wished.

" The Duke and his guests were still lingering in the dining-room after dinner, when one of the river-keepers came up to the Castle and delivered a message from the head fisherman, in the following words:

" ' Stevenson's compliments to your Grace, and Stevenson's mither's deid; but if she disna swell we'll burn her the nicht.' "

Auld Alec of the Creeshy Mill had been very quiet all the evening, quite unlike his usual habit, but he now chimed in:

" I was up at the big cairn the nicht, Dominie, and as luck wad have it I landed a troot of aboot a pund-and-a-half there, and thinking o' the reasons why these cairns were built set my mind back to a tale I once heard.

" As maist o' ye ken, these cairns nooadays are used maistly as a means o' reaching far into the river wi' yer fishing line, withoot having to wade and wet yer feet, or for diverting the water so as to make a stream; but in the auld days they were built to enable the tacksmen to work their cairn nets, and many a big haul o' fush they made.

" There was Auld Rob o' the Trows, who was tacksman doon at Makerstoun lang syne, and he came o' a hardy race o' fishermen and keepers. The story goes that Rob on one occasion had set his nets after a guid flood had brought up a fine run o' salmon, and he made a great haul.

" Rob was asked what his catch had been, and his answer was that he didna rightly know, but he did know that a cart was going all night to take the fish in to Kelso, and that it took him three days to drink ' the lave o' them ' ! "

" Aye, aye," said Wullie Veitch, with a wistful sigh; " thae were the days, an' sawmon were easier got then than they are noo. But I'm thinkin' we wad be wiser tae tak' doon oor rods, an' gang awa' hame, for there'll be nae troots gotten here the nicht, nor the morn's morn, wi' a' this rook aboot."

Then the little gathering broke up, and we each went our several ways, without regrets at the poverty of our sport for once in a way, as we knew there would be other and more fortunate nights when reels would ring out their music, and the creel strap would press heavy on the shoulder. For the angler is seldom a pessimist.

BALLADE OF THE OLD POACHER

There's waur things than the fireside glow
   At hame this cauld and bitter night;
Outbye, the wind blaws, full wi' snow,
   Across the moon, and dims its light;
But here is comfort, wi' my bright
   Sweet smiling Nancy in the nook:
Relaxed, at ease, I hae delight,
   Snug by the fire, wi' pipe and book.

There's some, where swirling waters flow,
   Gae wi' a cleek, and flaring light,
Wi' stealthy tread, and cunning throw,
   Snatch gleaming saumon silv'ry bright.
Eh, sirs! it's no' a bonnie sight—
   The bleeding fush, the furtive look.
But me? I'd raither rest at night
   Snug by the fire, wi' pipe and book.

There hae been times when I wad go
   Wi' Jock, or Dave, some clouded night,
And burn the water, to and fro,
   Tae seek a fush or twa that might
Our daring and our skill requite,
   Then, hapless, feel the cruel hook.
That's bye; and now I take delight
   Snug by the fire, wi' pipe and book.

Envoy

Nae mair for me on winter night
   Tae seek the fush, by hook or crook;
There's greater pleasure and delight
   Snug by the fire, wi' pipe and book.

AT THE MONKS' FORD

THE ANGLER DREAMS

Down by the river, dreaming,
Upon a summer's day,
I saw the great trout gleaming,
In sun-veined depths, at play;
They had no care, of hook or snare,
Their life was bright and gay—
And I was there a-dreaming,
Upon a summer's day.

Down by the river, dreaming,
Upon a summer's day,
With dancing sun-rays, beaming,
The trout made holiday;
The scene was fair, I did not care
To mar their happy day—
For I was only dreaming,
Upon a summer's day!

CHAPTER XIII

AT THE MONKS' FORD

IT was June, and a hot and sultry day. I had
been fishing from early in the afternoon until
evening. The river was very low, some of the runs
being mere trickles of water, and, although I had
not many trout to show in my creel, every one had
called for my utmost skill and craft before it was
safely landed. Besides the fly, I had employed
less pleasant lures in my endeavours to capture the
wily trout, even to using a minnow in the bright
clear waters, and I tried my fortune too with several
" creepers " which I had found by careful searching
below the stones in a shallow, much to my surprise,
as they were some weeks later than I had found
them in any previous year. " Creepers," carefully
fished with in the proper season, can be a very
deadly bait in the hands of an expert, but they are
elusive and fearsome-looking creatures to handle
withal.

However, poor as my sport had been, there was
still the evening rise to look forward to, and I was
confident that I should be able to augment my
catch before I reeled up my line and betook myself
home. So I sat me down on a grassy knoll under-
neath an ancient beech, where I could command
a view of the pool above the Monks' Ford, and up
to " The Bush aboon Traquair " on the opposite

bank. Signs of the first of the rise would be seen,
I thought, from my point of vantage, as soon as
the moths and sedge-flies began to float by and
under " The Bush."

Just below where I was stationed there is a
shallow ford across the river, quite passable in
low summer water by wading knee-deep, and,
except in floodtime, through which a horseman
may easily go. Tradition has it that the ford was
used by the monks of Dryburgh and of Melrose
when they visited each other, and this is readily
believable, seeing that the ancient abbey of Melrose
co-existed on a site but a mile or two up the
river, on the right bank, with Dryburgh Abbey,
which flourished a little lower down on the opposite
side.

Those religious men of ancient days must have
been fond of angling, not only as a pastime and
recreation, but as a means of obtaining wholesome
food, for no fairer or more productive reach of a
river did ever angler ply his wand upon than that
between and adjacent to the two abbeys.

Imagine, too, what the fishing must have been
like in those days, before the reclamation of the
lands for husbandry had set free the pent-up waters
of moss-hag and moorland bog, and when the river
floods probably took as many days to run down
as they now take hours. Verily, it must have been
an anglers' paradise, and such monks as had the
true sporting flair, and did not fish merely for
the replenishing of the pot on Fridays and Fast
Days, must have enjoyed some great and glorious
experiences, and, incidentally, have forgotten oft
to say their prayers at the appointed times, when

the fish were taking. But perhaps the worthy abbot would remit any penances due on that account when he saw the cooks bring great platters of appetizing fish into the refectory for the breaking of his fast.

Thus my thoughts as I sat in the quiet shade of the old beech-tree that summer eve, half drowsing in the sultry warmth, with now and then the sleepy drone of a beetle winging past, and the birds quietly chirping in the woods behind ere settling to rest for the brief summer night, while I almost forgot that I was waiting for the evening rise to begin.

. . . .

I had thought I had been quite alone, but surely I hear a deep voice singing, and I can distinctly make out the words, although the accent appears a little foreign to my ears, and such as I had not heard in any of my travels. He sounds a jovial sort of fellow, singing with a sort of chanting voice:

> " Ere the morning sun is high,
>   Crimsoning the eastern sky,
>   Forth to the field of labour, I
>   My way do wend;
>   A benediction here I give,
>   There counsel sinners how to live,
>   And oft the dying I do shrive
>   From sin to fend."

With the dense wood behind me, a tree-clad hill across the water, and the murmuring river in between, it was difficult to locate the position whence the singing came, but on looking down the river I observed two strange figures in the middle of the Monks' Ford. They were wading sturdily across, the water washing over their knees, and appeared to be attired in cassocks of a coarse grey cloth, the skirts of which were kilted high and held in place away from the water by their girdles. Slung across their shoulders were leathern sandals. Their tonsured heads were bare, the cowls which usually covered them being flung back. Indeed they were a quaint picture, and at once I seemed to be back in the early part of the sixteenth century, gazing upon some of the old monks from Dryburgh. Was I dreaming?

One of the monks carried a long staff, which was of some aid to him as he waded; but his companion appeared to be carrying a fishing-rod in one hand, while with the other he held a sort of hoop, on which were strung many trout of great size and weight. I found out later that the hoop was a long rod cut from a willow-tree. The rod had been pushed through the gills of the fish, the ends being brought together and fastened to form the hoop—an ingenious way to carry fish, it seemed to me, in the absence of a creel or pannier.

It was the monk who had the fish who was so jovially vocal, and, even as I gazed, with open-mouthed wonder and surprise, at the spectacle before me, he burst forth again with his deep and melodious voice, continuing his chant-like song:

> " For my earthly body's sake,
> Alms, and gifts of cheer I take,
> Then back to the cloistered fane I make
> My homeward way;
> Content that ere the setting sun,
> Another day its course has run,
> My Father's work has been well done—
> And thus I pray."

By the time he had finished his stanza the two of them had reached my retreat under the beech-tree, and with grunts and sighs of relief they flung themselves down on the dry grassy bank and proceeded to dry their feet and replace their sandals.

It seemed a curious thing to me that they had not observed my presence, and I might have been non-existent for all the notice they took of me. Then the fisherman of the two began to address his older companion:

" 'Tis right glad I am, brother Thomas, that I have such a goodly string of fish for my labours, since on the morrow we hold the vigil of Saint John the Baptist, and the refectory will see no flesh-meats set down before the brethren by good brother John, our most excellent cook.

" But we shall feast full well on these fat trout which I have here, and the reverend father the Abbot would as lief dine on a good fish from the Tweed—whether it be trout or salmon—as from a slice from a haunch of venison or a roast of the good Scots beef."

" Aye, brother Peter, thy trout are wholesome fare, and sustaining and satisfying food, prepared as the excellent Friar John doth prepare them, sprinkled with the fresh-ground oaten meal ere he plunges them into the hot butter, as I have seen him do, and then served up deliciously brown and sizzling hot from the fire. Aye, and the brethren are fortunate to have so skilled a fisherman amongst them as thou art, brother Peter, to replenish the larder with good fish when needs be for days of fasting," responded his companion.

" Well, well, brother Thomas, it is but fitting

that we should follow in the footsteps of Our Lord's apostles, and acquire some skill in the capturing of the finny creatures of the waters, as well as being fishers of men."

" That is true, Peter, and thou followest well after the founder of our Holy Church at Rome. Yet it is not given to many of us to attain the skill thou hast in alluring fish from the streams, however successful we may be in converting pagan souls to the true faith."

" Ah! good Thomas, thou flatterest me; but I was not ever as wise as I now am in the art of fishing with an angle.

" I will tell thee from whence came much of my knowledge of this useful and pleasant art.

" As a mendicant friar thou wilt know I have travelled many a long and weary road, not only in this rugged country of the Scots, but also in the richer lands of England, in the southern parts of which country this art of fishing with an angle is much better understood.

" On one of my journeys I sought shelter and companionship for a time with the holy men at Winchester, where there is indeed fishing of rare quality, and trout of a lustiness in the streams there such as I have ne'er seen any to compare.

" And it was there that I read a little book, in which was set forth *A Treatyse of Fysshynge wyth an Angle*, writ by one Dame Juliana Barnes. In sooth, brother, the good dame was wise in all that pertaineth to this craft of fishing with an angle, and she doth give instructions in the making of a rod or angle wand such as I do carry here. Thou wilt perceive it hath a hollow butt, of hazel, and also a second piece of the same supple and strong wood, with a fair shoot of blackthorn, tapering from a splice, to the top. 'Tis light of weight and full nimble to throw a line with.

" We are told how to make a fishing line by twisting together hairs got from the tail of a horse, and moreover how to fashion hooks from steel, and eke to simulate flies of divers sorts. And even this night I have been successful with a fly she nameth, that has wings of the buzzard feather bound with hemp.

" Solomon, in his parables, sayeth that a good spirit maketh a flowering age—that is, a fair age and a long.

" Thus is it written in the good dame's *Treatyse*, and she asks this question:

" Which be the means and the causes that induce a man unto a merry spirit? And, truly, to her best discretion, it seemeth good disports and honest games in which man joyeth without any repentance after. The best of them all, to her simple discretion, is fishing, called angling, with a rod and a line and a hook.

" Aye, brother Thomas, Dame Juliana doth recommend the disport of angling as a means to a long and holy life."

Here the holy man ceased his discourse, and quietude reigned around us, while all nature seemed hushed as the shadows lengthened into the peacefulness of the gloaming.

But the mendicant friar was still full of his beloved fishing, and he commenced his chanting song again, in a subdued voice, which was tuned in harmony with the murmur of the river and the gentle rustling

of the leaves of the beech-tree overhead. Thus he
sang:

> " In summer oft sweet peace I find,
> And contemplate with quiet mind
> The gracious gifts of God most kind,
>   Down by the brook;
> And with my tapering angle, I
> Go forth to fish with dainty fly,
> To fill a creel with trout I try,
>   By hook or crook."

There was silence again for a brief space. Even
the twittering of the birds, as they sought a roosting-
place for the brief summer night, ceased to be
heard, and only the melancholy hoot of an owl
some distance away vibrated on the air.

" I am thinking, brother Thomas, that this
disport of angling bringeth us great joy, and we
are nearer to our Maker here in the woodlands,
by the river with its ceaseless song of praise, than
in the hurly-burly of life amongst men. There are
wars, and rumours of wars, and e'en yesternight
did a friar come hot-foot from the south, bringing
disquieting news of armed men marching towards
our fair domains, with intent to plunder.

" Ay, dio mio! 'Tis a strange world, and I have
seen strange happenings in my brief day. Here in
this sweet paradise on earth we seem far from strife
and jealousies, and can, for a time, forget there
are such hideous things as rape and pillage and
covetousness.

" But we must hence, and seek our cells in Melrose,
or we shall need do penance for our worldly pursuits.
Ay, ay, ay! Thomas; thou dost look awearied,
and wouldst be happier resting thy old bones in a

dry cell, rather than here where the river-mists will soak into thee and give thee rheums and pains."

And with this the two of them rose to their feet, Thomas picking up his staff, and Peter his rod and heavy string of fish; and as they disappeared along the woodland path the deep voice of Peter could be heard continuing his song, and these were the words which I heard—words which seemed to fit the circumstances so well:

> " When the evening shadows fall,
> When the curfew tolls its call,
> When silence creeps down over all,
>   And all is peace;
> Then retiring to my cell,
> I wait the call of compline bell,
> To sound o'er all its tuneful knell,
>   And bid strife cease."

The rich voice faded gradually away as the monks ambled along the woodland path, and I saw no more of them; but I felt very mystified, and could not understand why they had ignored my presence. I sat up and looked around me, wondering. The gloaming was merging into the mirk of night, and it was without doubt a late hour.

Just at this moment I heard the squelch of wet brogues and waders coming down the path, and one of the local anglers came on the scene.

" Guid evenin', sir," he said. " I hope ye hae had guid sport. I'm thinking the rise is ower for the nicht, but the troots didna take sae badly, either."

I asked if he had met anyone on his way down,

but he replied that there was naebody up abune but himsel'.

Had I been dreaming while the evening rise was taking place? It was all very strange.

So I packed up, and went home, and was soon abed.

GRAYLING IN TWEED
AND TEVIOT

o

CHAPTER XIV

GRAYLING IN TWEED AND TEVIOT

THERE is a local legend that there have been grayling in the Tweed and the Teviot since the days when the monks inhabited the many abbeys, now picturesque ruins, which flourished long ago in the south of Scotland. A member of an ancient family, which has been settled on the Borders for many generations, once told me that the grayling were originally introduced by the holy men at Jedburgh Abbey. The fish were kept in stew-ponds there, and one day, at a time of flood, the ponds were overwhelmed, and their banks broken down, whereupon the grayling escaped to greater freedom into the Jed Water. From the Jed to the Teviot is an easy swim; and, as Tweed weds the Teviot not so far away at Kelso, it is not surprising to find these fish in Tweed also.

On what historic grounds, if any, my informant founded his statement I do not know. He was quite emphatic about it, and he was a learned man. Anyhow, he was a graduate of a university, and would therefore not be expected to make statements based only on legend, and hope to be believed. However, it is significant that grayling are more numerous in the Teviot than in the Tweed; and, again, they are more plentiful below Kelso than above that point in the main river. This may be partly because there is much water in Teviot and in the lower reaches of the Tweed which suits their habits—they love quiet deeps, with a clean gravel bottom. There are, of course, many such places above Kelso; but in general the waters are more streamy and rapid - flowing the farther you go up-river.

Most of my personal experience of fishing in the Tweed has been above Kelso; but I have never caught many grayling, and do not recall ever taking more than one in any day, when fly-fishing for trout.

Anglers at St Boswells, of long experience, will tell you that the first grayling ever heard of in their district was caught near Mertoun Mill in the 1880's, and it was such a rare capture that none of the local fishermen could say what description of fish it was.

One who has fished the Teviot frequently below Ancrum tells me that if he had a good catch of fish he was sure to have several grayling in his creel. At other times he might have an odd one, or none at all; but his opinion was that some parts of the Teviot held a great many grayling, running from half-a-pound to three-quarters of a pound in weight as a rule, with now and again one up to a pound-and-a-half. My informant told me of seeing the farm-labourers catch many big ones in the summer evenings, and they were so little esteemed that the men would throw them on to the river bank to rot, as they would an eel, which is detested by most Border fishermen.

One old gentleman had great sport amongst the

grayling in the autumn, fishing with the fly. The flies he used were virtually sea-trout patterns, and he fished with two of them on a fine cast.

Another successful fisher would visit the Teviot at Nisbet in the winter-time. His method of fishing was with the worm and a float—he fished the swims in the fashion of a Thames angler fishing for bream or perch or other coarse fish. He did not reckon his catch by the pound, but always spoke of the stones of fish he caught!

There was an old Tweedside fisherman I knew, with long experience, who I thought could give me some information, and on one occasion when I was out with him, fishing, I asked him if he had ever caught grayling in Tweed.

"Ou, aye, whiles!" was his laconic reply; and, when I had got so much out of the usually silent and dour Wullie, it was not difficult to encourage him to tell me more of what he knew of *Salmo thymallus*.

But, after all, he had not much to tell.

"Whiles," he soliloquized, "I hae gotten them wi' the flee when fishin' for troots, baith in the simmer an' in the back-end; an' I hae whiles gotten them on the mennit [Border Scots for minnow]; but mair often wi' the worm in a flood-water, at a' times o' the year."

Wullie was a man of great experience as an angler of all descriptions and styles, on Tweedside. He was what might be termed an unattached professional—that is, he made a great share of his precarious living by fishing, and selling what he was fortunate enough to catch. To use a slang expression, he fished " on his own hook " and was beholden unto no man. Consequently, he was an independent being. His great failing was a fondness for lifting his elbow too much, in the local inn; but in his own estimation he felt himself as good a man as ever threw a fly, and the equal, when on the water, of any man there who could afford to pay his hundreds a year for the rent of a salmon-fishing. There are still a few left of these strange and independent ne'er-do-wells in the villages and hamlets of Tweeddale.

Although these men, generally speaking, are not averse to a little poaching when it can be done with safety, they are usually expert anglers, and can tell you all the choice bits of water for miles around where a trout, sea-trout, or salmon is likely to be met with. So, if you should ever be fishing the Tweed, and find that fish are dour and will not take your lures, leaving you at a loss what to do, get hold of a man of Wullie's stamp and he will advise you, since he knows the best patterns of flies to use on any given day, merely from long association with the conditions in his particular neighbourhood, and having little else to do or think about. Hence I thought I might be able to glean from Wullie some information about the grayling and its habits, as far as Tweed was concerned. But the pot-hunting professional angler is seldom much of a true naturalist; his main ambition is to fill his creel, so that he may exchange its scaly contents for the shining siller.

Wullie's opinion of the grayling as a sporting fish was the common one of most of the local anglers. The fight these fish give is usually a brief one, and they do not indulge in the exhilarating leaps into the air, and the wild rushes for freedom, that a good trout will make. The mere fact that the grayling does not show itself much when hooked, but bores away into as deep water as he can reach, constitutes a defect in the estimation of the angler who has fished for trout and sea-trout most of his angling days.

That there are more than enough grayling in the Tweed is amply shown by their frequent capture with various lures, and it would appear that they are increasing yearly in numbers, to the detriment of the trout-fishing. It is significant that Stoddart makes no reference to grayling in his *Angler's Companion*, from which we may assume, I think, that they were so few in his time that he did not deem them worthy of mentioning as a sporting fish, although he devotes a whole chapter to pike, perch and eels, the first-named of these being very numerous in the Teviot in his time.

I have known several anglers who have taken grayling in the upper reaches of Tweed, fishing in the evenings, during June and July, with the fly, and the fish were in good condition. One was caught which was full of mature ova. It weighed three-quarters of a pound, and was a noteworthy capture, as these fish usually spawn in April or May. In that particular year the spring had been a very late one, and cold. I had news the same year of a grayling of $2\frac{1}{2}$ lb. being landed so far up the river as Innerleithen, on a fly.

A Galashiels angler confessed to me that he had caught grayling some miles above Melrose, fishing with that illegal lure salmon-roe. He never used any other bait, he said, so he was sure it was the

" paste " he had got them with. I once found a dead one below Bemersyde. It had apparently been badly bitten by an otter, and when alive must have scaled very nearly 4 lb. It was an exceedingly handsome specimen. I saw an angler take a very nice one of 1½ lb. with the dry fly on the Dryburgh water. The Ravenswood keeper some years ago informed me that he had known of several grayling being caught there, but always by bait-fishers, and never, as far as he knew, on the fly. I have, however, caught them with the fly, in the spring months, fishing from the Gledswood side of the river, and once or twice I have landed them at Mertoun, where, a few years ago, a grayling of two pounds weight or so was brought ashore when the waters were being netted for gravid salmon for the hatchery which Lord Polwarth had at that time.

To sum up such scanty information as it is possible to obtain, it would appear that in the higher reaches of the Tweed—that is, from Melrose upwards—grayling are only occasionally met with, and are regarded as rare and unusual occupants of the trout-fisher's creel, and more or less as an accidental addition thereto. In the mid reaches of the river they are more often caught, while in the lower waters they are said to be quite plentiful.

The usual rule regarding the habits of *Salmo thymallus* is here exemplified, for this fish does not evince much desire to run up the waters, inclining more towards a liking for the lower part of a river, where the waters often run still, and broad, and deep.

The Teviot in many places is well stocked with grayling, the long deep reaches of this river, which glide along slowly and then ripple off on to clear gravelly shallows, being favourable to their natural habits. There are few anglers who habitually fish the Teviot and have not frequently caught them either with the fly, worm, or minnow. Many stretches of the Tweed are also eminently suitable for harbouring these handsome fish, which are such favourites with many southern anglers. The river abounds with swift streams, rushing down into deep pools, with quiet eddies and backwaters, and there is many a length of deep flat water running over sharp clean gravel bottoms—just such quarters as the grayling loves to haunt.

I have already pointed out that the grayling in Tweed and Teviot are said to be increasing numerically. Whether this is a desirable state of matters for Tweed anglers would seem to be a debatable question. Looking at it from the trout-fisher's point of view, it may be said that on other rivers—on some of the Derbyshire streams, for example— grayling are alleged to have increased to such an extent that they have almost ousted the trout from their former haunts, the latter fish becoming scarcer, and many of those caught in the height of the season being ill-conditioned, pointing to the supposition that the grayling are getting the upper hand of the trout in their fight for food and life— a case, possibly, of the survival of the fittest.

There is undoubtedly a curious prejudice against the grayling. It is not looked upon as a desirable fish for the Tweed by many anglers. There is plenty of natural feeding for the fish in this river, which could doubtless stand the strain of countless numbers of additional inhabitants. In any case, a heavier stock of grayling would provide good fishing for the angler in the late autumn and winter months, when, in the first place, trout are going off condition, and, later, during the closed season for trout.

But, on the other hand, the lessees and owners of salmon-fishings, large sums for which are now asked and readily obtained, might have a real grievance were the grayling so numerous as to bring out many anglers for them during the autumn salmon-angling season. The ardent grayling-fisher might interrupt their sport, as I have seen thoughtless and selfish trout-fishers do before the close time became law, and nothing is more calculated to rouse the ire of a salmon-fisher than to see a man go over his water before him with a trout-rod, wading, as often as not, and disturbing the water for which much gold has been paid.

As long, however, as salmon and sea-trout fishing are the great features of the autumn angling in the Tweed, so long will the presence of grayling in any considerable numbers be looked upon with a certain amount of disfavour.

It will always be the opinion of many anglers that neither for its sporting properties nor its culinary value can the grayling compare with the more lively trout or the migratory salmonidæ, and it will be time enough to encourage and stimulate their increase in the classic river when the more desirable fish are becoming extinct beyond all hope.

That such a sad fate will never befall the silvery Tweed must be the fervent prayer of all who have fished its waters, and may the time be very far distant when there will be never a clean-run salmon, or a plunging, rushing sea-trout in its streams, to thrill the fisherman as he hears the reel whirring out its music to the accompaniment of a line fast running out.

As Auld Wull would put it: " A grelling is a' weel eneuch if ye haena gotten onything else; but gie me a guid saumon or a bullie, or e'en a dacent louping yallow trout, an' I'll no ask for ony better fush ! "

A BORDER RAID

THE BORDER RAIDER

The reiver rode the Border land
  O'er moss-hag, flood, and fell;
And with him went his gallant band,
For a maid there was, and for her hand
  He sought his love to tell.
          And they sang a song, as they rode along,
            In the mists of the morning grey;
          " O far we ride, for a Border bride,
            —So chaunt we all our lay—
          Our life is brief, but a Border chief
            Will take whate'er he may."

The reiver rode o'er the marches far,
  By moor and fell and flood;
When darkness came, and the evening star,
With the crescent moon, shone from afar,
  At the castle gates they stood.
          And they sang a song, nor waited long,
            At the gates in the gloaming grey;
          " O far we ride for a bonnie bride,
            —So chaunt we all our lay—
          Our life is brief, but a Border chief
            Will take whate'er he may."

The reiver from the Border land
  Passed through the castle gate;
He seized the maid, whose heart and hand
For his own he claimed, and with his band
  Rode homeward with his mate.
          As they galloped along, they sang a song
            In the mists ere the dawn of day;
          " O far we ride, with a Border bride,
            —So chaunt we all our lay—
          Our life is brief, but a Border chief
            Will take whate'er he may."

CHAPTER XV

A BORDER RAID

IT is always an adventure to fish a river or stream you do not know, and on which you have never thrown a line before. You may be skilled in river-craft, you may know a great deal about catching salmon or trout; but on a water he does not know even the most experienced, without guidance from some better-informed angler, feels at a disadvantage the first time.

One morning at breakfast-time my father announced that he had been offered a day on a well - known stretch of the River Liddle, below Newcastleton, and I was to accompany him and try for a salmon. So I was all agog for the day to arrive, as it would be new ground for me. My salmon-rod, and reel and line, were at once examined to see that all was in order, and flies suitable for a small river sorted out.

So we set out one fine September evening for Newcastleton, and put up for the night in the small inn there, that we might be ready to make an early start. We were up betimes, breakfasted well, and then were driven in the dogcart down the river for several miles to the water we were to fish in.

We were told that a few salmon were up, as a flood about ten days earlier had induced them to run; but when we saw the low and bright condition of the river we felt we should be very fortunate indeed if we took a salmon that day. However, the angler always hopes for the best. A brilliantly clear sky and strong sunshine did not augur well for success.

We were warned, moreover, that a notorious poacher had been killing salmon on the waters in the neighbourhood, and it was said that he either used rake-hooks or worm when he was on the war-path. As like as not, said our informant, he would have all our water fished long before we got started.

My senior having a greater fondness for trout-fishing—and, wise man, perhaps better judgment than I had in those days—elected to fish for trout only, and we arranged to take the pools and streams alternately.

After fitting up our rods we strolled quietly along before deciding on our starting-point—we had a long stretch of the river at our disposal—and as we came round a bend suddenly we came upon a man with a stout salmon-rod, intently fishing a fine pool, obviously with the worm. When he espied us he quickly reeled up his line, and scrambled hastily up a steep bank, being soon out of sight.

Liddesdale in the days of old was a notorious haunt of Border reivers, and the " thievis of Liddisdail," to quote Maitland of Lethington, were so arrogant

" That nane may keep
 Horse, nolt, nor scheip,
 Nor yett daur sleep,
 For their mischeifis."

It seemed to us that the poacher we had seen must have been a direct descendant of a Border thief, and we were none too pleased to think that the water for a mile or two down had been disturbed before we had thrown a line on it.

However, there was nothing for it but to make the best of things as they were, so, after seeing my father make a beginning in some nice streamy and broken water—it being a bright clear day and the river low, he fished with worm—I passed on until I came to a likely-looking pool, and commenced operations.

I fished the pool most carefully, with a small " Jock Scott " fly, but touched nothing, nor did I have even a rise. At the tail of the pool I reeled up and waited for my senior. When he came along he had two or three nice little trout, and was quite pleased with the start he had made.

There was a long stretch of streamy if somewhat shallow water after this, which I left alone, and passed on to another pool, where I had no more luck than I had before.

I always think that salmon-fishing is more tantalizing than fishing for trout. The salmon-angler may sometimes fish for several days on end and never touch a fish, although he knows there are fish there. But with a low clear water, and if the angler be restricted to the fly as a lure, he is often a disappointed man at the day's end.

It became rather monotonous, thrashing pool after pool, wielding an eighteen-foot rod, and no encouragement from seeing a fish move. Every now and again my father and I met. Each time he smilingly exhibited his bag, with a few more trout added, and I began almost to wish I had brought my trout-rod with me instead of the salmon-rod.

Lunch-time came round, and with it a little adventure, for as we were looking for a desirable place whereon to rest awhile—we had just climbed over a stone dyke into a pasture-field—an irate bull espied us from some distance away, and with a lashing of his tail and lowered horns he came straight for us. Needless to say we were back over the dyke in double-quick time, and we were no sooner in a place of safety than the bull had reached the other side of the dyke and was bellowing resentment and defiance. We easily dodged him, however, by making a short detour.

Luncheon over, and to the river again. I had fished for perhaps half-an-hour when I did at last move a fish in very deep water. Incidentally I may mention that in the Liddle there are some very dangerous holes, and the angler has to exercise great care when wading. He may be walking on a flat rock, barely covered with water, and then come to a sudden cleavage in the rock, and he is on the verge of a hole of many feet deep. An angler equipped with waders, and fishing alone, would have little chance to save himself were he to step over the edge of one of these dangerous traps.

It was in a place of this description that I rose my first fish. He came up from the depths with a lunge, flung himself into the air with one wild bound, and was off. A small fish of eight or nine pounds I should say he was, but a very ugly red one that must have been in the river a long time. I felt somehow that I had not missed much, the fish was so uncomely. Sour grapes? Perhaps.

And so to other pools, changing my fly to a "Butcher," or a "Durham Ranger," or a "Turkey

Wing," in the hopes of inducing a fish to respond to my blandishments, but the afternoon wore on and never a fin showed itself. Nor did I even see a trout rise to a fly anywhere, although every now and again my father reported the capture of " a few more small trout; nothing big," on his worm bait.

We had arranged for the dogcart to pick us up at the bottom of the water, to take us back to Newcastleton, where we were to catch a train home to St Boswells. The time left, unfortunately, would not allow of our fishing on into the dusk, which would probably be my best chance for a salmon. Our last half-hour had arrived when I came to a splendid pool, the best I had seen that day. Here, I thought, if there are fish to be had at all, I should get one.

It was a long deep pool, with a fair amount of stream to the far side, and, commencing at the top, I fished all the water I could reach in most careful fashion, in the hope of redeeming a fruitless day.

A loud whistle from the road at the top of the brae which sloped to the river called my attention to the fact that time was up, and I saw my father had already taken down his rod, and was removing his waders. He beckoned to me, calling out that we must get away at once in order to catch that train at Newcastleton. But I had to have one last desperate cast.

So with the last cast of the day my fly went well out, and I worked it round towards the side of the pool. Just as I was about to reel up there came a tremendous boil, and then a great silver flash in the air from a leaping fish. I had missed him—a salmon of well over 20 lb. I was certain. I might have got him to rise again, had I had the time, but I had to leave him, to my chagrin. Had I hooked him I expect I should have cared little about the train we had to catch.

A disappointing day? Well, I had no fish to show, but I had had a new experience. Still, I made a mental vow that should such another occasion arise I would not be tied to catch a train at the crucial time in the evening. My father, while being sympathetic about my ill-luck, could not refrain from chaffing me about my lost " big 'un." He was quite pleased with himself, for he had quite a decent basket of trout.

A BUNCH OF HEATHER

HEATHER IN LONDON TOWN

Heather white for fortune
The purple for the true;
Wear it, and be steadfast
As the hills whereon it grew.

You send me heather from the misty moorlands,
Purple and white, as autumn's early morn;
Faint-scented as the breeze, which o'er the uplands,
Wafts nectar sweet, and makes man feel new-born.

Do whaups still mourn their loves in eerie wailing,
O'er Eildon where it slopes to Bothendene?
Home muircocks to their mates when day is failing,
'Midst heather on the hill yont Halidean?

In fancy once again I climb the Eildon,
And gaze around the everlasting hills—
To Cowdenknowes, and Bemersyde, and Dunion,
And Cheviot with its glens and sparkling rills.

See, winding through the vale, past scaur and shingle,
Fair storied Tweed, a silver streak, gleams gay;
With which the peat-stained Leader hastes to mingle
By Old Melrose, where monks erstwhile held sway.

Oh! shall we e'er again, when blooms the heather,
Walk hand-in-hand across the breezy moor;
As in lang syne we often roamed together
And wandered o'er the hills towards heaven's door?

Heather white for fortune,
The purple for the true;
Wear it, and be steadfast
As the hills whereon it grew.

233

CHAPTER XVI

A BUNCH OF HEATHER

THERE are times when the fisherman will wish to get away from the low-lying lands where the big river flows, and lift his eyes unto the hills, and the freer spaces of the high lands, since there are hill burns where he will find trout in good numbers, even though they be small in size, in comparison with the fish to be found in the broad river. There is something, too, in the spirit of the hills and moors which you will not find in the valleys, something which gives a greater sense of freedom, of being less hemmed in, and farther from the madding crowd.

The heather-clad moors were brought to my door this morning, vicariously, by a postman with his loud double knock. The moors of my memory are hundreds of miles away, in the north, and if I would actually see them I must hie me there, as Mahomet to the mountain.

Yet the contents of the parcel the postman brought to me awoke vivid memories of the moors and the heather, and the sparkling streams that I know of, that have their origin in the mist-swept hills. In my parcel was a brace of grouse, their poor limp bodies —which only a few short days before had been alert with sprightly life, gaily strutting on the wild heath—reposing on a bed of that heather which had been life and shelter to them since they were fluffy little " cheepers."

Just a bunch of heather, and a brace of grouse. That was all, but what memories they aroused.

My childhood's days were spent within a brief walk of the moors. I was born almost on the fringe of a moor. The first breath I drew must have been of the pure air of the upland country. As a boy I roamed about a farm where the heather actually grew on the rougher pastures, and beyond the farm there was a great tract of moorland which, to our young minds, appeared to stretch into the infinite. If we climbed the hill behind the farm there were always other hills beyond, and heather purpling far away to the horizon.

As we grew older, and began to explore the country, we discovered its boundaries miles away to the north, where the hills sloped into a fair valley, dotted here and there with little lakes, which brightened the landscape like glittering gems. Moreover there were tiny rivulets tumbling down the hillsides, gathering strength and volume as they progressed, and clad with such verdure of woodland trees as, in our philosophy, we had not dreamed of in our bleaker world. But then, we were very young, and our travels had been very circumscribed.

.   .   .   .   .   .

Come with me for a ramble over the moor on a day early in the summer, and we will go over some of the old well-known ground where we wandered so often in our youth.

We enter the moorland proper by the appropriately named Moorgate, a wide road that climbs right into the heather, by way of the Devil's Bridge, crossing a deep ravine, and thereafter rising gradually up a winding and steep acclivity to the very heart of the moors. It is pleasant enough here now, with the summer just newly come in, and the great expanse of heather newly tipped with a soft green growth dearly loved by the grouse, and the ferns and brackens freshly uncurled; but in the wintertime it is a bleak and awesome spot.

But we will turn aside from the road and the Devil's Bridge, and seek the track through the heather, which passes along the ridge to our left.

There, down below, is the little dingle where the wild roses grew in great profusion when we were schoolboys, and I have recollections of rising early on June mornings and rambling there before the sun had dispersed the dew from the yet unopened buds; and I have culled bunches to take home to my dear mother, whose pleasured smile of thanks was enough to send me off to school with a cheerful mien and gladness in my heart. Ah, well! I am old enough to tell of it now, but I should have been shy of any of my schoolfellows seeing me carrying home a few sprigs of the poet's eglantine. For boys are like that.

Verily are the hills everlasting, for, to us short-lived mortals, they appear to change not. See, in the dell, even now, there are some wild roses in bud, which soon will be displaying their pale pink blossoms to the rays of the sun in the rose-hued dawn.

We move ahead, and come to an old ruin, which has served its purpose at one time as a shepherd's hut, or a gamekeeper's shelter. It is now a mere heap of stones, overgrown with lichens and heath,

It will be forty years since I sat here alone on a day of bright sunshine, in the beginning of May, and a cuckoo alighted on that heap of stones within ten feet of where I rested. The beautiful bird bowed towards me with outspread wings, and "cuckoo-ed" for very life. It gave me a strange and wonderful thrill. Although she was so close to me, the bird's call was very mellow, deep-throated, and pleasing. I cannot imagine what it was doing there on the wild moor, far from any woodland trees, unless it had tired in its flight and dropped down there to rest its pinions.

As we advance we must have a care to keep to the track, since there are grouse still nesting on the moor, and we surprise more than one pair that rise with a loud cry of "Go back! Go back!" alarmed at our invasion of their peaceful domain. They do not fly far, and sail gracefully down to a patch of bright green, which later on will provide them with delectable feeding in the shape of the luscious purple bilberries. Where bilberries grow, grouse are not far off.

The further we go, the wilder does the moor become. In harmony with the landscape, curlews are wheeling high, ever calling their weird and plaintive cry as they sweep in graceful curves up and down over the boggy lands.

We have reached a high point on the moor, and we seem, as indeed we are, far from the haunts of men. Yonder is a "cairn"—just a heap of stones—which marks the spot, so legend says, where the bodies of two boys were found, dead from exposure, having lost their way when crossing the moor on a wild night of winter. The place is known by the name of " Two Lads " to this day. And we see from here, also, a pillar erected to commemorate the place where a Scots packman—on his rounds, visiting the scattered hill farms, peddling his wares, like Autolycus—was set upon by wandering gypsies and the life beaten out of him, it is said, in revenge for an insult to one of their tribe. Robbery was a more likely motive for the deed, as the man was known to carry a fair sum of money with him.

We reach the summit of the moor, and are enchanted with the view beyond, revealing to us many a pleasing glimpse of tarn and stream. In our descent we pass a spring, the ultimate source of a beautiful hill burn, which, not many miles lower down, has often given us a day of sport with the rod, and pleasing creels of small brown trout.

There are evidences round the spring that the grouse come here in considerable numbers for watering purposes. Soon the young birds will be on the wing, gathering strength from day to day, and in a few short weeks will be driven to the slaughter at the butts, when the peace of the moor will be destroyed by the noise of beaters and sharp reports from the guns of the sportsmen.

We have had a pleasing ramble, and we retrace our footsteps to the lower ground again; but we change our route a little, so that we may strike the main road, such as it is, where it will be much easier walking on its comparatively smooth surface, than striding over heather tufts. We pass on our way a small clump of fir-trees, beside which stands a lonely birch—the only trees, and rather wind-swept and stunted, for many a furlong. In bygone days we have often seen three or four magpies in that clump of firs, and they would chatter loudly at us as we passed.

We make a call at the little dairy farm, as we were wont in the old days, in the hope of there being a glass of buttermilk for us, and we are not disappointed. The same family is still in the farm-house, but a younger generation now reigns where their forefathers dwelt beyond remembrance. And we wonder how they have always managed to eke out a livelihood on the bleak moor, and keep their sturdy independence so long.

And so home, which we reach as the sun dips down behind the skyline, sending out golden rays from the horizon, like glittering sword-blades, when the blazing orb has sunk from sight.

There were many ravines and glens running down our side of the moor—places of mystery and charm, bird-haunted and full of wild and busy feral things, and, so said the old folks, where elves and fairies, warlocks and bogles dwelt. Few human beings ever set foot there, but sometimes we were privileged to go picnicking in one or other of those glens, which usually resolved itself into a rather wearying hot scramble over fallen trees, and around boulders, beset maybe by damp quagmires, and now and again the necessity of a leap across the little stream.

Which reminds me. There was a boy, still in his teens, who was invited to join one of these rambling parties. The plan was to traverse a wild glen for a mile or two, a glen with a brawling brook scampering its course to the valley down below, and over-hung densely with unpruned trees and brushwood, its steep sides being clothed with ferns and bracken.

A BORDER BURN

[*page* 240

There was no properly defined path, and possibly the only wayfarer the place would see in the course of a summer would be an occasional gamekeeper. The top of the glen opened out to the heather, where there was a small farmhouse, and thither the little party was bound, to partake of an *al-fresco* tea, on a terrace in front of the farmhouse, where there was a commanding view of the country below.

There were some dainty and charming girls in the party, and the youth attached himself as attendant cavalier to a sweet young damsel who had captivated him with her smile, and twinkling humorous eyes, which were shaded beneath a fascinating, broad-brimmed sun-hat.

On they gaily plodded up the glen, scrambling, climbing, and sometimes splashing in the brook, for it was rough going.

At one point the only way of progress round a deep pool was to be compassed by holding back a branch of an overhanging tree. The strong man of the party grasped the bough, and most of the ramblers had passed, stooping, safely through, when it came to the turn of the laughing little damsel of the bright blue eyes, and her attendant youthful swain. The lady went first, but just at the crucial and psychological moment the branch slipped from the strong man's hold; it swung back, and caught the little lady a glancing blow, which swept her off her feet and, alas! plump into the pool.

There was no danger, of course, but the young man, in alarm and distress, jumped down after the lady, and lifted her out—none the worse for her involuntary dip, but very, very wet. She was hurried off to the farmhouse, and the farmer's kindly wife found a change of clothing for her until her own garments had been dried. The youth was also very wet; but no one troubled about him. His tweeds soon dried on him as he moved about.

Ah, those youthful days! And the pairing off on the road home. Naturally the maid and the boy drifted together, and the walk home in the peace of the summer dusk was an idyll of innocent youth, in which silence was more expressive of their happiness than any speech could be.

They were very young, and at parting, greatly daring, and full of a strange and indefinable rapture, the youth took the hand of the shy maid in his own, and raised her finger-tips to his lips, to impress upon them a reverent kiss. Romance is surely made of such circumstance.

Eh? No, they did not marry and live happy ever after. He went to a far country, and she found another romance.

THE OLD GROUSE'S WARNING

" *Kek-kek! Kek-kek!* " *the cock-grouse cried,*
And each cheeper craned its crest
Towards a mound, where, in his pride,
Their lordly chieftain they espied,
His pinions earthward pressed.

" *Come gather round, my downy dears,*
List, while I speak ye fair,
For ye are raw, and wanting years,
Your callow youth has known nae fears,
Ye've aye been free frae care.

" *Safe hae ye roamed the muir at will,*
Nor hawk, nor stoat, nor fox
Hae ye e'er seen upon the hill—
The laird's man harried them until
He drove them frae the rocks.

" *Syne fill your craps wi' heather tips,*
And pick the blaeberries sweet,
While frae the running well that drips
Its moorland dews, tak mony sips,
Tae cool ye in the heat.

" *For sune ye maun fly long and strong,*
Since, when the heath's in bloom,
Loons frae oot-by will be along,
Wi' noisy guns, whose deadly song
Rings like the crack o' doom.

" So get ye strong upon the wing,
Learn weel tae fly full fast,
That when bloodthirsty gunners fling
The lethal lead, that gies death's sting,
Ye'll maybe dodge the blast.

" Tak tent by me ! regard my age !
Lang did I here abide;
The beaters oft hae roused my rage,
Driving me o'er where guns engage
In screenèd butts tae hide.

" But I've won through, and still I'm here,
Tae counsel and advise;
So, when the rabble charge your rear,
Fly strong, be bold, and show nae fear,
Fly high as ye can rise."

" Kek-kek! Kek-kek! " the cock-grouse crew,
Then, with a whir o' wing,
Flew down to where the bilberries grew,
Syne crammed his crap till his neb dripped blue,
Then squatted 'neath the ling.

SEPTEMBER TROUT AND SPATES

SEPTEMBER PASSES

Frost in the air, and the morning mist
Mellows the fruits that the warm sun kissed;
And, seen in the copse, through filmy haze,
Browning brackens are a russet blaze.

Its purple glory fading away,
The heath on the hill is ageing grey;
And gone is the droning hum of bees,
That sipped its nectar sweet, to the lees.

Bare are the fields where the ripened grain
Late bent to the breeze like golden rain;
Black are the berries, by brambles borne,
In the hedgerows bedewed at wake of morn.

Eagerly down the fisherman's track,
Wand held in hand and creel strapped a-back,
The angler goes forth, hopeful he may,
Be laden with trout ere ends his day.

Hushed soon will be the song of the reel,
Gone be the angler with rod and creel—
But winter will pass, and spring come amain,
Then ho ! for the trout, and the reel's song again !

CHAPTER XVII

SEPTEMBER TROUT AND SPATES

THE heather is past its best on the moor, and its purple richness is greying towards decay. The lush growth of bracken on the lower heights that rise from the back of the wood is beginning to blaze with its rich brown of autumn, while the tips of fern-fronds in the dell are blackened here and there with the early night frosts.

Elms, beneath the shade of which the angler has rested from the torrid heat of the sun that glared down in the midday hours of the summer past, are now beginning to fade, and some of the leaves are already turning to a saffron-yellow. The beeches have put on a russet hue, and their crisp leaves rustle sibilant music as they quiver in the gentle breeze of this Indian summer.

Only a few weeks ago the river was but an attenuation of its usual self, dribbling in narrow channels where now are plunging streams. For the summer has been an arid and thirsty one. Where that rippling sheet of water is now, as like as not holding a whitling or two, or maybe a sea-trout up to five or six pounds, was a waste of channel stones, bleached white with the scorching rays of the sun, and fringed by a luxurious growth of grasses, a forest of reeds, and golden marsh-marigolds gleaming in the sunshine.

September had scarce been ushered in when came the rains, heavy downpours, not so welcome to the farmer with corn still ungathered from the higher lands, but a pleasing sight to the fisherman who has been sighing for a cleaner river free from flannel-weed and slippery mosses, and for more water and room to fish in with the hope of creeling trout, or even an odd sea-trout or salmon. For the angler's time is short now, and the end of the angling season for trout looms near, when the rod and line must be laid aside until spring comes round again.

The fishing day is becoming abbreviated by mid-September, and from about ten in the morning until four or five in the afternoon is the time when the angler is likely to creel trout with the fly. An hour or so later the sun will be sinking, and the temperature at the river's edge may drop to freezing-point. Often, after a day of clear sunshine, you will see the sky flush to a faint pink or rosy hue as the sun goes down, deepening into purple in the far distance, with a thin misty haze appearing on the far-away purple like the delicate bloom on exotic fruits. On such evenings comes the chill of early autumn, when the first frosts warn the angler that the end of the season is near at hand.

At this time of the year, if there has been a freshet or spate, the angler will in all probability see a sea-trout or two rising at the tail of a stream, or in a run fringing a pool; and many a one have I captured in the greying of the evening, before the darkness falls—fish up to five or six pounds, which fight as only sea-trout can fight for freedom, running hither and there, leaping high in air, inducing in the angler's heart a tense feeling of dread that he surely will get away, until at last the gamest of fish gives in, and is tailed up the gravel.

We have had welcome floods these early September days, and the river is in fine fettle for fishing, toned down to a good clear colour, slightly tinged with the stain of peat maybe, but all the more pleasing a sight for that to the angler hoping for the due reward of his labours.

Some of the local experts, who know every stone in the river, and every likely spot for a trout to lie, have been doing well, especially one or two adepts at spinning a natural minnow in a heavy water, and some fine trout have been taken by this means.

Before the waters cleared the usual crowd of worm-fishers were busy with strong tackle and big worms, hoping to secure a basketful while trout were still flood-sick and had the " glaur in their een," as they say, fishing within a few feet of each other in the backwaters and eddies. Few of these men ever appear on the waterside except when the river is " drumly " and flooded, and some of them obtain huge catches. They are verily " coarse " fishers for game fish, and seldom appreciate properly the more æsthetic side of angling with a fly, and the use of tackle so fine that the angler gets the maximum of sport, while the fish has also a chance to win the fight. Again, if you watch some of them carefully, as I have done, there is a suspicion of salmon-roe being used as bait by one or two furtive and notorious pot-hunters. But more anon of this fishing during autumn spates with bait. To-day we are out to fish with the fly, in a water suited to it.

So, with optimistic hopes two of us saunter down

the glen riverwards betimes in the forenoon. The Doctor is no great fisherman, a busy practice precluding his spending much time on the river; but he is with me to-day to try his skill and increase his knowledge of the gentle art to some degree. For he declares that this fishing game is a fascinating and healthful one, and a fine anodyne for the nerves in this fretful age of speed.

We decide to fish up the water from below the Monks' Ford, and having plenty of time to spare we do not hurry as we select our flies and tie them on the cast.

We are fishing the wet fly, so our first selection, and always a good one for an autumn water, is the Partridge Spider, and we decide that an Olive Dun and a Greenwell's Glory will complete a cast that should do good execution. Our casts are identical, our rods are the same length and of similar make, so we begin on an equal basis—and so to our dysporte.

Old Tom Stoddart knew this stretch of water well, and often killed a creelful of big trout here. It is a long stretch of open water, not too swift-flowing on the side from which we are fishing, but deepening into the centre, with good streams close in to the far bank. The bed is gravel, and it is easy to wade, with ordinary wading stockings, to near midstream, where you can cast right and left as you wade up the river, when the water is not too high. The conditions to-day are all that can be desired.

There being plenty of room for two rods to fish fairly close together, we commenced near each other, and were each rewarded by rising trout with almost the first casts we made. I had trout of half-a-pound and three-quarters of a pound, and the Doctor was delighted when he killed one of four ounces or so for his first fish. It was amusing, after a while, to hear him call out:

" Look here, old chap, what are you fishing with that you are getting all the big 'uns, and I am hooking only the small fry? "

I assured him that he was using the same kinds of flies as myself, and that it must be a matter of luck; or perhaps I knew, from greater experience of the water than he had had, exactly where to find the trout lying, and I consequently wasted fewer casts of the fly. But to mollify him I suggested an exchange of rods, and let him use mine. It made no difference. He still went on capturing the small ones, but plenty of them, and having sport that was not to be despised by a tyro who fished very few days in the season.

Meanwhile my own sport was good enough for a time. The trout were in a taking mood for about three hours, when they ceased to rise to the fly. None of the flies we had used came amiss, but on the whole that old favourite in a fairly heavy water, the Partridge Spider, was the best. My creel contained sixteen or seventeen trout, weighing 10 lb. in all. The Doctor's catch more than equalled mine for number, but the aggregate weight was much less. But we were well satisfied with our few hours' sport, and had as many fish as we wanted for the day, so we wound up our lines, took down our rods, and sat for a while below the old beech-tree above the ford, discussing various matters connected with trout and trout-fishing, while we smoked our pipes contentedly.

One subject we spoke of was the question of bait-fishing for trout in the autumn, particularly with the worm when the water is discoloured. This mode of fishing is of course of a vastly different nature from that in vogue when the water is low and clear. Clear-water worm-fishing upstream requires as much skill, many aver, as does fishing with the fly, if trout are to be caught; but no skill or art is needed to pull trout out of a muddied pool on a large hook baited with a lob-worm.

Anyone who is wont to resort to the river frequently cannot fail to observe the large numbers of men out with the rod at flood-times, and to the really skilled angler with refined ideas of what is right and fair to the trout, and the well-being of sport with them generally, the sight of large trout being literally dragged from the water by crude fishing is abhorrent.

There may be some amongst these anglers who may develop into more accomplished and discriminating fishermen. Doubtless there are some who may in the course of years learn to appreciate the charms of the finer methods of angling and become adepts at fly-fishing, clear-water worm-fishing, or even " creeper " fishing. We all have had to serve our apprenticeship to the craft, and the love of riverside sport and life grows upon us with the years, and the experience years of fishing brings to us.

Some may never get beyond the lob-worm and muddy - water stage, and still deem themselves sportsmen; and one must, I suppose, make allowances for differences of taste. As Pope has told us:

> " 'Tis with our judgments as our watches, none
> Go just alike, yet each believes his own."

There is another aspect of the question, besides the sporting view.

If you will come with me to the river, let us say, any day in October before the legal close time begins, provided there has been a flood of some size and the waters are beginning to fall, I will show you at least a score of men and boys all within sight, and all busy with strong tackle and worm as bait. Nearly all these fishers have heavy baskets of trout, and some of the creels are very heavy indeed. Many a sea-trout and salmon is taken by these men and illegally retained. For this latter reason alone I knew one proprietor who stopped all fishing for trout on his water when the nets were taken off the river-mouth on 15th September. This was erring on the severe side, perhaps; but if all bait-fishing were to cease with the month of September there would be an immense improvement in the stock of trout eventually.

As examples of the catches made, I knew one local man who took 33 lb. of trout one late autumn day. He was a little ashamed of it, and tried to keep it quiet. Another day, a party of five rods took 125 lb. in all; and I have known pot-hunting fishermen to hawk trout from door to door, their creels containing some splendid trout, as far as size went, although the same could not be said of their condition.

A large proportion of the trout caught with bait in the autumn are useless for sport, and unfit for the table. They assemble at this time below the weirs, and in the pools below the streams, awaiting the opportunity to reach their spawning-grounds. Many are gravid trout in advanced condition, avid for food, but with little strength or inclination to fight or run when hooked. Consequently they are easy prey to the pot-hunter, whom you may see standing in the same spot for hours hauling fish from a flooded and discoloured river.

My experience has been that trout full of roe do not rise readily to a fly, even in a favourable water, in the autumn. I have fished with the fly in late September and in early October, and noticed this time after time. But for choice I have always fished the streams and runs, leaving the pools and quiet eddies rigidly alone.

There was one day—entered in my diary—for example, on which I took sixteen trout, all plump, well-conditioned and lively fish. When I arrived home I opened them all up and examined their ovaries. Not one of them contained ova far developed; and although their colouring was not so fine as that of summer-caught trout, yet they were desirable fish, fit for the table, and had given me excellent sport.

This one example supports an opinion I have long held. Fly-fishing alone should be permitted towards the end of the season, if the stock is to be maintained, as the majority of the fish caught thus would be either barren ones or males not mature, while the heavy spawners would be left to replenish the river with young trout.

The establishment of the close time for trout in Scotland was a great step in the right direction; but if it were to commence on 1st October, instead of the present date, who can say but that a great improvement in the trout-fishing would result in a few years' time?

RUSSET AND GOLD

There is a fragrance in the frosty air,
And, dancing in the sunlight, golden-brown,
The leaves, loosed by the breeze, float slowly down,
To lay a russet carpet everywhere,
Inwove with glowing crimson, passing rare—
Beads from the rowan, fruits from hawthorn strown—
Like magic robe from far-off Orient throne:
Yet never man wove pattern half so fair.
E'en so the setting sun this autumn day,
In final blaze of crimson-spattered gold,
Shines forth in beauty born of day's decay,
Ere night's dark mantle falls o'er stream and wold.
But night recedes, and dawns another morn;
And winters die, that new years may be born.

VISCOUNT GREY, K.G.

(Author of FLY FISHING)

Obiit, 7th September 1933

He joyed to see the fecund Earth unfold
  Its wondrous glories, as, with rod and line,
  He plied his blameless sport with skill so fine—
Of which his graphic pen has nobly told;
And, like the Saint of Assisi of old,
  He charmed the feathered songsters from the tree;
  While, where he trod abroad, o'er moor or lea,
E'en creatures of the wild with him were bold.

Yet, when stern duty called, at the behest
  Of that dear Homeland which he loved so well,
A statesman's part he played, nor craved due rest
  Though o'er his vision a dire twilight fell.
    Now is the fisher Home, his sport is o'er:
    The statesman's fame shall live for evermore !

"THE LURCHER'S" LAST
CAST

CHAPTER XVIII

"THE LURCHER'S" LAST CAST

MY old fishing friend, who was known to all the local fishers as "The Lurcher," was beginning to look rather frail last autumn, and his once-active figure had begun to stoop somewhat, while the long limbs, which erstwhile loped along in such an untiring way, seemed to lag as he strolled by the river.

Yet "The Lurcher" was still apparently as keen as ever he had been, and, when Tweed was in fishing order, you would be sure to come across him within a short radius of the burn-foot, casting a light fly and fishing far, or spinning a minnow in that inimitable way he always had. His right hand had become claw-like with grasping a rod so much, and seemed to be part of the rod as he made his cast.

His sight was not so good now, and he had a difficulty in ascertaining what kind of fly was on the water. This was not such a great handicap, after all, as he seemed to have an intuition of what fly was most likely to hatch out at any time of the year, under given conditions of wind and weather, and he was seldom wrong in his judgment. It was a faculty he had acquired through a lifetime of observation when fishing.

The winter had been a hard one, and severe on

the old folk. The changeable weather—now a hard frost, and then a sudden reverting to mild and muggy weather, or days of cold rain—was very trying to tender chests, and to rheumy joints. "The Lurcher" had had many a wetting in his fishing days, and as the years grew on him he felt the damp affecting his limbs, and rheumatism, that dread trouble of the labourer class, had him in its painful grip.

Yet when spring came round again he could not be kept away from the river. Indeed, if he were out-of-sorts and feeling pain he would brave it out with:

"Hoots, I'll be a' richt once I can get down tae Tweed an' hae a cast or twa at the troots. If only we could get juist the richt day for't."

Then if a propitious angling day came round you would see the old fellow on his way "down the glen" to the river, with his rod over his shoulder and creel aback, and with waders and brogues already donned. He would be as happy as a boy, and confident that a few hours at the waterside would set him up for weeks, and the exercise would loosen his joints and relieve the pains. If he succeeded in landing a few trout—and he seldom returned with an empty basket—his face beamed with a delight it was a pleasure to see.

But the Scottish spring is a treacherous time, and the old man had been compelled to spend most of it indoors, and sometimes he had to keep to his bed.

When the warmer days of summer came he seemed to gather strength, and I saw him several times on the river, always with a rod in his hand, casting his fly mostly from the bank, as he was now too feeble to wade into the river, especially where there was any current to contend against.

There was one day, however, when he had become venturesome. I saw the old man wade cautiously and with some timidity into the shallows above the islands. Here the river is wide, but suddenly converges into a powerful stream deflected by the islands into a narrow gorge known as " The Battery."

Somehow I thought he was over-estimating his powers, and, making a pretence of changing my cast of flies, I remained near by, watching him. I noticed that he appeared to be confused, as if the rippling, dancing water, with the glint of the sun upon it, had dazzled him or made him dizzy. He dropped his rod, and put his hand up to his head; but by this time I was at his side, and took his arm, or he would have fallen. We retrieved the rod, and I gave him support until we reached the bank, where he recovered, and explained that he had only just come over a wee bit dizzy-like, but was quite all right again.

However, after a rest, I deemed he were wiser to go home, and, pretending that I did not think it was any use fishing until much later in the evening, I persuaded him to accompany me, as I was going home, and could see him safely to his own door.

Some weeks later I was passing " The Lurcher's " cottage and saw him in his garden, pottering about amongst the flowers he loved. In former years he had been an enthusiastic gardener, and in such time as he could spare from work and fishing he cultivated flowers and vegetables, with such success that he always captured his share of awards at the village flower-show.

So I asked him how his garden was doing this year. He shook his head, and said he doubted if he would have anything worth showing, as he hadna been able to do much gardening of late.

Inevitably the ruling passion of his life was uppermost in his mind, and the conversation soon veered round to fishing.

" I was thinkin' we'll be havin' a pickle rain: my pains hae been gey sair the day. Aye, aye! If Tweed cams doon in spate there should be a guid chance o' some fine creels o' troots. I'm thinkin' it wad juist be graund tae hae a cast again, and tae hear the reel ringing wi' a guid troot hookit."

And sure enough, down came the rain before the dawn of another day—a steady downpour which brought the Tweed down in spate, and cleansed the river-bed; but, like most summer floods, it soon waned, and the water was clearing by the afternoon of the next day, leaving it in fine condition for fly-fishing.

I had taken my rod to the riverside, more as an excuse for a stroll, and to see what the water was like, than for serious fishing, and when I got to the burn-foot, and looked up the river, I espied " The Lurcher " fishing the runs below the islands, made by what we knew as " Little Tweed." The river here is divided into three streams by two islands, the centre and main stream forming the beginning of a fine pool, and it was at the head of this pool he was fishing. Many a time had I seen him wade deeply in and fish it with the minnow, and many a trout of noble size and quality had I seen him play there with consummate skill.

I sat down on the grassy river bank and watched the old man hook one or two small trout, and then, with a wistful look, he slowly reeled up his line, waded over the shallow side-stream and, with an effort, climbed up the bank and sat down, rather heavily, beside me. I noticed that he was shaking and evidently a little distressed, so I suggested that he should rest himself for a wee while, and then we would saunter back up the glen together.

"I doot the troots are gettin' ower muckle feedin' on the river-bottom the noo. They are no' risin' tae the flee ava; an' it stands tae reason they maun be gettin' lots o' ither guid fare—minnows, worms, caddises, and thae kind o' creeper things.

"But I thocht I wad juist like weel tae thraw a flee, and mebbe kill a troot or twa for a fry for the guidwife. The auld body is gey fond o' a troot whiles; but for my ain pairt I dinna often eat them; I'd sooner catch them ony day. For a' that, they are a dainty tae mony folk.

"Aye, aye," he murmured on, "but I doot my fishin' days are gey near done."

I tried to assure him that he would yet be able to catch a few now and again, but he shook his head sadly, as if inwardly he had an intuition that his time was almost come to hang his creel by the wall for the last time.

And so it happened to be. I had not seen him about, either in his garden or at the river, for some days, so I made inquiries from one of his neighbours one day when I was passing by, and was told that the old man had had another of his bad turns. His heart had given way, and he was very feeble and confined to bed.

It was probable, it seemed, that " The Lurcher's " long figure and fishing-rod would never be seen on the river again; so, one day, when I had been out for a few hours' fishing, I thought it would gladden the old fellow if I took my catch and offered it to him.

How pleased he was! He gazed at the few fish as they reposed on the platter, and murmured something about the speckled beauty of them. Then he began to speak to me.

" Ech, sir, I doot I hae thrawn my last flee. But I hae nae regrets, for mony happy days—aye, and nichts—hae I spent on Tweed, an' mony a bonnie creel o' troots hae I carried hame.

" Ye'll mind weel, sir, the summer nichts on the Gateheugh, and yon grand Boat Pool up abune? Ech! the bonnie troots we hookit yon—one o' the sweetest bits o' the bonniest river in oor beautiful country.

" It is hard tae leave it a', sir; but maybe whaur I'm gaun there'll be compensations. Yet, after a', can ye imagine paradise wi' onything sweeter tae gie than a summer day—aye, or a summer nicht— on Tweed, by Bemersyde or Auld Melrose?

" Ech, aye; an' how the birdies would chirp and sing in one tremendous burst of heavenly music as the dawn's glimmer cam' ower Bemersyde Hill: I wad never wish to hear a grander chorus.

" But we live oor day, and pass on, and maybe we dinna appreciate fully a' the blessings we hae until we canna enjoy them ony mair, and the end draws nigh."

The old man was wearying himself, so I got up, and, saying I might look in to see him again soon, took my leave.

"Guid nicht, sir; an' thank ye, again, for the bonnie troots. May ye hae mony a guid creelfu' yet, for in the ordinar' way o' life ye should hae mony years ahead o' ye," he said, as I took his hand in good-bye.

That was the last time I saw him alive. His soul passed while he slept that night. He must have been dreaming of Tweed in his last moments ere his weary heart failed, for as he lay there in his last sleep his face had a happy smile upon it, just as he was wont to look when he was at the waterside, with everything going well, and trout rising to the fly, in the way an angler loves.

"Sleepe after toyle, port after stormie seas,
    Ease after warre, death after life, does greatly please."

"The Lurcher" had made his last cast; and, as was his wish, he lies where one could fain hope he still hears Tweed's murmuring song.

CLOSE TIME

Just one more cast !
For soon my reel, in silence,
With rods and gear, must all be laid away;
Now here I muse, sad, in my sportive dalliance
   This autumn day.

Just one last hope !
'Twould set my heart a-singing
If some great trout—to crown my season's sport—
Would seize my fly, and rush—my reel a-ringing
   In merry sort.

Reel up the line !
Ah ! swift, snug in the ingle
With tale and book, chill winter's days will flee !
Till spring's bright sun shall tempt me forth to angle
   Again, with glee.

BOOKS ABOUT SCOTLAND

THE ELUSIVE RIVER
By GEORGE PRATT INSH
A roving survey of the Clyde from Daerhead to the Tail of the Bank.
Illustrated.   **6s.** *net*

WADE IN SCOTLAND
By J. B. SALMOND
A fascinating book dealing with the old roads and bridges so closely connected with General Wade's command in Scotland during the Jacobite risings.
Illustrated.   **5s.** *net*

LOVAT OF THE FORTY-FIVE
By W. C. MACKENZIE
The life of one of the most intriguing figures of Jacobite Romance—
Simon Fraser, Lord Lovat
5s. *net*

LANDMARKS IN SCOTTISH LITERATURE
By GEORGE PRATT INSH
A history of Scottish literature from medieval times to the present day.
5s. *net*

SAINT ANDREW OF SCOTLAND
By PROFESSOR R. K. HANNAY
The story of Saint Andrew, the patron saint of Scotland, is told in this book in a way that gives it interest to young and old alike. How many Scots at home and abroad know why Saint Andrew is their patron saint?
Illustrated.   **2s. 6d.** *net*

IRREGULAR BORDER MARRIAGES
By "CLAVERHOUSE"
The romance of the runaway marriages on the Borders and the general interest in the world-famous smithy at Gretna Green are amply proved by the number of visitors to that spot each year. The author has compiled a most interesting history of the Gretna "priests" and their ceremonies around the historic anvil. The book is illustrated with portraits of many of the old "priests," and other unique pictures of great interest.
Illustrated.   **5s.** *net*

THE MORAY PRESS: EDINBURGH & LONDON

THE
SCOTTISH NATIONAL
WAR MEMORIAL

WITH AN INTRODUCTION BY

Sir IAN HAMILTON, G.C.B., D.S.O.

Royal 4to.   Boards, with cloth back.   **15**s. *net*
Bound in half morocco. -   -   - **30**s. *net*

This handsome volume contains 46 whole-page illustrations, most of which are IN COLOUR.

Throughout the Memorial the artists and craftsmen have employed colour, which is an essential part of the beauty they have created.

Without colour it is impossible faithfully to portray that beauty. In this book, this has been done in print for the first time.

The Weekly Scotsman :

"An exquisite volume profusely illustrated. It is a volume in the possession of which every Scot must feel a special pride."

The Glasgow Herald :

"These illustrations reproduce more truly than any we have seen the majesty and nobility of this tribute to the spirit of Scotland."

Edinburgh Evening News :

"A beautiful book. The illustrations bring the War Memorial very near to one."

THE MORAY PRESS: Edinburgh & London

MOUNTAIN DAYS IN THE ISLE OF SKYE

By

J. E. B. WRIGHT

Demy 8vo.   Cloth.   Illustrated.   12*s.* 6*d. net*

A real book for climbers and mountaineers.
The author is the founder of the "Lakeland
Mountain Guides," and was the first professional
guide in this country.   For the last ten years
he has been the head guide of the English
Lake District area.   He has made over 1200
ascents of different mountains in Central Europe
and the British Isles.   He has made over 2400
rock-climbing ascents in the Lake District.
North Wales, the Isle of Skye, Switzerland, the
Bavarian and Austrian Tyrol and the French
Alps.   Nearly 8000 mountaineers have engaged
his professional services.   His book is a record
of actual climbs in Skye, with ample details of
vital importance to mountaineers.   There are
over sixty pictures, reproduced from beautiful
photographs, and his narrative is interesting,
well-written and absorbing to all who have
made, or would like to make, the many ascents
with him.

THE MORAY PRESS: Edinburgh & London